Also by William F. Ha

Dialogues of the Great Things of Brazil
(Diálogos das grandezas do Brasil)
Translated and annotated by Frederick Arthur Holden Hall,
William F. Harrison, and Dorothy Winters Welker
University of New Mexico Press, Albuquerque, 1987

Spanish Memory Book: A New Approach to Vocabulary Building
William F. Harrison and Dorothy W. Welker
University of Texas Press, Austin, 1990

Spanish Memory Book: A New Approach to Vocabulary Building,
Junior Edition
William F. Harrison and Dorothy W. Welker
University of Texas Press, Austin, 1993 (out of print)

Portuguese Memory Book: A New Approach to Vocabulary
Building
William F. Harrison and Dorothy W. Welker
University of Texas Press, Austin, 1996

Intermediate Spanish Memory Book: A New Approach to
Vocabulary Building
William F. Harrison and Dorothy W. Welker
University of Texas Press, Austin, 1997

Perfect Pronunciation, By Jingle!

William F. Harrison, Ph.D.

Illustrations by Sophia Varcados

iUniverse

Perfect Pronunciation, By Jingle!

iUniverse books may be ordered through booksellers or by contacting:

iUniverse
1663 Liberty Drive
Bloomington, IN 47403
www.iuniverse.com
1-800-Authors (1-800-288-4677)

ISBN: 978-1-4759-2273-8 (sc)
ISBN: 978-1-4759-2275-2 (hc)
ISBN: 978-1-4759-2274-5 (e)

In Memory of

**Dorothy Winters Welker,
my mentor and friend**

Contents

Acknowledgments

I want to thank the hundreds of Midwesterners I pestered to learn how they pronounce the words contained in this book and my college students who accidentally made me aware of the severity of a virus that is impeding communication throughout the country. A special thanks to Douglas Kwiecinski, barista extraordinaire, for sharing his astute awareness of how people pronounce words.

I would also like to thank those who read multiple versions of this document: my late brother, Dr. Earl Harrison, and my son, Jeff, as well as Francine Zephier, a longtime educator and my close friend for a half century, and Melissa Birks, a reporter for the *Rockford Register Star* I met during the excavation of the juvenile *T. rex* Jane. Additional thanks goes to Bill "eagle-eyes" Feldman for proofreading the manuscript. I am particularly grateful to Gail Jacky, director of the Northern Illinois University (NIU) Writing Center, for not only editing countless versions of the manuscript but also providing me with technical assistance in formatting the book.

Additionally, I would like to thank the administrative assistants (Lynne Meyer, Rita Miller, Renée Kerwin) in NIU's Department of Foreign Languages for going out of their way to help me with this project. Finally, I would like to thank the Department for its financial support in defraying some of the cost of the illustrations.

Introduction

Perfect Pronunciation, By Jingle! offers a unique method by which speakers of Standard American English can expand their vocabulary rapidly and avoid mistakes in pronunciation. This book provides most, if not all, of the acceptable pronunciations for a word, and all of these can be trusted in any situation. We at times include British pronunciations so you can recognize people who are trying to impress you by adding a European flavor to their tone.

The author hopes that by using jingles to model pronunciation patterns, you can enjoyably learn to pronounce more than 350 words in just a few hours.

The book also makes readers aware of a virus that has crept (nearly undetected) into the language and affects the pronunciation of millions of speakers of American English. This virus causes a speaker to change voiced consonant sounds such as **b**, **d**, **v**, **g**, **z**, and voiced **th** (ð—as in ei**th**er) at the end of words into their voiceless counterparts **p**, **t**, **f**, **k**, **s**, and voiceless **th** (θ—as in **th**in).

If you have this devoicing virus, you end up "marrying the mo**p**" rather than the "mo**b**." When completely worn out at night, you "go to be**t**" when "be**d**" is the intended destination. Your loa**th**ing (loð ing: extreme disgust) of gambling dissipates into mere loa**th**ing (loaθing: unwillingness), and off you go to the casino. On the road, you hit "buc**k**" after "buc**k**" instead of "bu**g**" after "bu**g**." Making the trip even more hazardous, your companion's "black eye**s**" turn into "black i**ce**." Once at the casino, the "fi**ve**" of your sure-to-win straight turns into a useless "fi**fe**."

I offer a test to see if you are a virus victim. If you are contaminated, I provide a quick and painless cure.

To accomplish my mission in *Perfect Pronunciation, By Jingle!*, I had to identify the devoicing virus and offer a cure, as well as overcome other seemingly insurmountable obstacles, many of which can be blamed on our archaic spelling system. Modern English spelling reflects Londoner speech of 1470s, which became etched in stone when William Caxton introduced the first English printing press in 1476. No wonder there are so many discrepancies between the written and spoken word in English. For this reason, every speaker of American English needs this book! *Perfect Pronunciation, By Jingle!* provides a method for quickly and enjoyably learning the pronunciation and meaning of familiar and unfamiliar words.

Eighteen Obstacles to Proper Punctuation

Think you don't have a problem with pronunciation? You may be surprised. Before we get to the jingles that will make up the bulk of this book, let's look at eighteen trouble spots that trip up many English speakers and make the jingles necessary reminders.

Obstacle 1: Where Is Standard English Spoken in the U.S.A.?

There is no standard pronunciation in American English. Unlike Spanish, Portuguese, and French, English lacks an academy of language that periodically harmonizes pronunciation and spelling so a word is spelled as it is pronounced. The closest we come to a national pronunciation is the pronunciation used by national news anchors, generally referred to as the Midwestern dialect. Stephen Bloom, a professor of journalism at the University of Iowa, in an otherwise scathing description of Iowans and their part in the 2012 presidential election, does admit that they speak English in Iowa. "You understand the words fine … (broadcasters, in fact, covet the Iowa 'accent,' since it could come from anywhere, devoid of regional inflections.)"[1]

William Labov et al. identify this dialect region as spanning from Rockford, Illinois, on the east to Pierre, South Dakota, on the west and from Minneapolis, Minnesota, on the north and Sioux City, Iowa, on the south.[2] In creating *Perfect Pronunciation, By Jingle!,* I have used the 4th and 11th editions of the *Webster's New*

---

[1] Stephen G. Bloom, "Observations From 20 Years of Iowa Life," *The Atlantic*, accessed December 9, 2011, http://www.theatlantic.com/politics/archive/2011/12/observations-from-20-years-of-iowa-life/249401/.
[2] William Labov et al., *The Atlas of North American English: Phonetics, Phonology, and Sound Change: A Multimedia Reference Tool* (Berlin: Walter de Gruyter GmbH & Co., 2006).

World College Dictionary, which shows the spoken American English most commonly used throughout the United States, as my main reference tool for identifying acceptable pronunciations. I have also consulted an array of other dictionaries, including those online.

My roots spread deep and wide in the dialect region, as I was born in Sioux City, Iowa; raised in Sheldon and Storm Lake, Iowa; attended college in eastern South Dakota; and have taught at a university just south of Rockford, Illinois, for the last forty-one years. Most of the mistaken pronunciations in this book are those I have made myself or have heard my students and colleagues make. In some cases, I have included pronunciations not found in dictionaries but common to the Midwest dialect.

Obstacle 2: First Isn't Necessarily Best

People believe that when the dictionary lists more than one pronunciation for a word, the preferred pronunciation is the first one. The dictionary, in fact, remains silent on how the order was chosen so as not to give preference to regional differences. Dictionaries until recently tended to favor Eastern Seaboard dialects by listing their pronunciations first. For instance, the first pronunciation listed for "forest" asked the reader to pronounce the word exactly like "**far**est." As a speaker of the Midwestern dialect of English, I was scarred for life when my English teacher, who had memorized the first pronunciation listed for every word in the dictionary, informed me that my pronunciation of the **for** in "**for**est," which sounded like number **four**, was the ignorant pronunciation and that "**far**" was how educated persons pronounced it. I have been vindicated by *Webster's New World College Dictionary*, which lists my pronunciation, "**for**est," first and "**far**est" second. Unfortunately, my English teacher died in 2003, so I will never have the satisfaction of showing her that my pronunciation of "forest" was, in fact, just as good as hers.

Obstacle 3: Age Matters

Even in Standard Midwestern English, age-related pronunciations can lead to misunderstanding. I was attending a family function when a young resident of Buffalo, Minnesota, informed me that her dog recognized the word "wok." I hadn't learned the word until late in life when a Chinese restaurant called Happy Wok opened in our town in Illinois. I then announced that my dog only recognized the word "walk." "But that's the word my dog knows," our friend replied. "Wok—w-a-l-k." It turns out that many young people pronounce **alk** words as **ak** instead of **aw**k, making no distinction between the **a** of f**a**ther and the **aw** of s**aw**. To them, **Don** and **Dawn** are identical twins.

Obstacle 4: What in the World Is a Syllable?

Words in English are made up of syllables, one or more, but no one is sure how we arrive at these divisions. We do know that each syllable has at its nucleus a vowel (**a**, **e**, **i**, **o**, **u**), a diphthong (two vowels making a single sound such as **ou** in **ou**t, the **ai** in **ai**sle, and the **ei** in th**ey**), or a triphthong (three vowels making a single sound such as **way** /uei/ and **wow** /uau/). Notice that in **way** /uei/ and in many other triphthongs and diphthongs, the **u** sound is spelled as **w** and **i** as **y**. Because they don't have a full vowel sound, **w** and **y** are called *semivowels*.

We also know that each word has a syllable whose vowel, diphthong, or triphthong is emphasized more than any other in the word. This syllable carries what is called, in linguistic jargon, *primary stress* and is shown in this book in bold capital letters. An example is "microbic" (mi·**CRO**·bic), an adjective meaning "tiny." If you shift primary stress from **CRO** to **MI** (**MI**·cro·bic) or to **BIC** (mi·cro·**BIC**), your listener will think you are talking about a tiny ballpoint pen. In words of one syllable (shown all in bold capital letters), the vowel, diphthong, or triphthong automatically carries the primary stress (**I**, **A**, **OW**, **WOW**, **CROP**, **RUN**, **MAIL**, **SHOUT**).

5

Notice that you can have a word made up of a single vowel (**A, I**), a single diphthong (**OW**), or a single triphthong (**WOW**), but you cannot have a syllable made up of just consonants.

Silent vowels (indicated by light gray letters) cannot form the nucleus of a syllable; for example, the final silent **–e** that simply signals either that the vowel that precedes it should be given a long sound—as in **MADE, SCENE, FINE, MOLE,** and **DUDE**—or that some ancient scribe decided that a final **e** flourish enhanced the word's appearance.[3]

Many words do have a syllable that carries some stress, but the stress isn't quite as strong as that of the syllable carrying the primary stress. These are said to carry *secondary stress* and are indicated in this book by plain capital letters. An example is the fish called "bullhead" (**BULL·**HEAD), in which **BULL** carries the primary stress and HEAD the secondary stress. Another word that has a syllable carrying secondary stress is "agoraphobia" (AG·or·a·**PHO·**bi·a), which means the fear of open spaces. The reason that AG· rather than ·or· is given secondary stress is because "agora" is borrowed from the Greek AG·o·ra (wide open marketplace). To make a Greek freak out, shift secondary stress from the AG to the GOR (a·GOR·a·**PHO·**bi·a).

Obstacle 5: The Deadly Schwa

All vowels in one environment or another lose their identity by becoming a schwa sound, represented in linguistics by an upside-down **e** (ə) and pronounced like the **u** in "fun" (**FƏN**), "thud" (**THƏD**), and "come" (**CƏM**). Vowels in an unstressed syllable are particularly vulnerable to becoming a schwa sound. A ripe example is "banana" (bə·**NA·**nə), in which the initial and final unstressed **a** are each pronounced as a schwa. In fact, an **a** in the final position of words with more than one syllable regularly is

---

[3] "Final –e" Middle English Spelling and Pronunciation, accessed November 15, 2011, http://isites.harvard.edu/fs/docs/icb.topic453618.files/Central/pronunciation/pronunciation.html.

reduced to a schwa sound, as in "lava" (**LA**·və), "flora" (**FLO**·rə), and "mama" (**MA**·mə).

The letter **e** in "insistent" is pronounced as a schwa (in·**SIS**·tənt), as are the **o** in "melody" (**MEH**·lə·dy) and the **u** in "album" (**AL**·bəm).

Even **u** and **o** in a stressed syllable can have a schwa sound, as in "pun" (**PƏN**), "up" (**ƏP**), "pup" (**PƏP**), "conundrum" (cə·**NƏN**·drəm), "come" (**CƏM**E), "some" (**SƏM**E), "love" (**LƏV**E), and "glove" (**GLƏV**E).

A schwa in an unstressed middle syllable is susceptible to not being pronounced. Take, for example, "every," which was once a three-syllable word (**EV**·ə·ry) when pronounced with care or in isolation (its *citation* form). When "**EV**·ə·ry" was pronounced in the flow of conversation (its *connected* form), the schwa in the middle syllable was so often omitted (**EV**·ry) that today the connected form has become the only acceptable pronunciation in dictionaries. The old pronunciation (**EV**·ə·ry) is only occasionally used in poetry when an extra foot is needed.

For the word "history," all dictionaries give **HIS**·tə·ry as the citation form, and some list its connected form "**HIS**·try" (pronounced "**HISS** tree"). If "history" repeats itself (pun intended), its current connected form will eventually replace the citation form just as **EV**·ry has replaced **EV**·ə·ry.

Perhaps if the Press had been aware of the tendency for schwas to be deleted in an unstressed middle syllable in connected speech, they wouldn't have been so critical of President George H. W. Bush deleting the middle syllable of "broccoli" (**BROCC**·o·li) when he announced that he wasn't "going to eat any more **BROCC**·li."

Obstacle 6: Spelling Pronunciations Muddy Waters

Ask anyone how to pronounce **H-I-S-T-O-R-Y** and they are sure to give you its spelling pronunciation: **HISS TOE REE**. *Spelling forms* are produced by treating each syllable as a separate word, thereby restoring a recognizable vowel quality to each vowel. The verb "isolate" (ɪ·sə·lāte) is another example in which people invariably give the spelling form—pronounced like the nonsense phrase **I SO LATE**.

Spelling forms can also result from sounding silent consonants such as the **t** in "often" and "valet." The Brits do pronounce these **t**'s (**AWF·tən** and **VAL·et**), so if you do, too, you are giving a European flair to your English.

Spelling forms also come from assuming that vowels, diphthongs, and triphthongs in unfamiliar words have the same sounds as those in familiar words. Moms inadvertently misguide their children by pronouncing the **au** in **M-A-U-V-E** like the **au** in **cau**se, **pau**se, and Santa Cla**u**s. **MAWV** is the spelling form, but the true pronunciation is **MOWV**, which rhymes with "cove." (Dads, unless they are the principal caregivers, are off the hook, as the following cartoon illustrates).

However, the spelling form of **au** in "ma**u**ve" (considered the "beastly" pronunciation by Charles Harrington Elster[4]) is so often heard, it is starting to trickle into dictionaries.

Obstacle 7: Pronouncing Definite/Indefinite Articles

Certain monosyllabic words switch the sound of their vowel based on the word that follows them. The **e** of the definite article "the" can be pronounced two ways. When "the" appears before a word starting with a vowel, it may be pronounced with a long **e** sound ("th**ee**" apple) or as a schwa ("th**ə**" apple). When it appears before a word starting with a consonant, it is pronounced as a schwa ("th**ə**" house).

When you pronounce the indefinite article "a" in isolation, you are sure to pronounce the "a" as the first letter of the alphabet, "A." But when "a" is pronounced in connected speech (e.g., "I bought **ə** pen, **ə** book, and **ə** table"), it generally becomes a schwa unless you want to emphasize the phrase ("I only bought **A** pen, **A** book, and **A** table!"). Notice "a" only appears before words starting with a consonant sound. For example, you would say "a house" but "an hour," since the "h" in "hour" is silent.

Before words beginning with a vowel or vowel sound, the indefinite article "a" becomes "an," as in "an article" and "an MBA" (pronounced **EM BEE AY**). When "an" is pronounced in isolation (its citation form), it sounds like "Ann" (Ann apple). In connected speech, the **a** of "an" is pronounced like a schwa (**ə**n apple), and in lazy speech, it is reduced to an '**n** ('**n** apple).

Obstacle 8: Silent Knight

Thousands of English words have one or more silent letters. We saw that word-final –**e** is often silent when it signals the preceding vowel has a long sound: **MADE, FINE, MOLE,** and **DUDE.**

[4]Charles Harrington Elster, *The Big Book of Beastly Mispronunciation: The Complete Opinionated Guide for the Careful Speaker* (New York: Houghton Mifflin Co., 2005), 306-307.

The **a** is dead in HEAD, BREAD, COCOA, COACH, and BEAN, and unstressed schwas (as in EVERY, HISTORY, and FAMILY) are dropping like flies. Other examples follow:

- The initial **k** in "knight" (KNIGHT), "knave" (KNAVE), and "know" (KNOW) is silent. But don't drop the **k** sound in "picture" (PIK·chur), or you will end up with either a water or baseball "pitcher" (PI·cher).
- The initial **g** is silent in "gnat" (GNAT) and "gnome" (GNOME).
- The initial **m** is silent in "mnemonics" (mne·MON·ics).
- The initial **p** is silent in "pneumonia" (pneu·MON·ia) and "psychology" (psy·CHOL·o·gy).
- The **t** is silent in "often" (AW·fən) and "valet" (va·LAY). The **t** is also silent in "notch" (NOTCH), "watch" (WATCH), and "catch" (CATCH).
- The **h** in "chord" (CHORD) is silent.
- Word-final −**b** is silent in "dumb" (DUMB), "bomb" (BOMB), and "numb" (NUMB).
- The **l** is silent in "calf" (CALF), "half" (HALF), "halve" (HALVE), and "yolk" (YOLK).
- The **s** is silent in "aisle" (AISLE) and "isle" (ISLE).

The word "wrestle" (WRE·stle) has three silent letters. Only the letters **r-e-s-l** are sounded.

Obstacle 9: Sound Switching

Sometimes speakers switch (transpose) sounds in a word, often with comical results. As we saw on the book cover, the tigress transposed the **s** and the **k** of "asked" (aksed), which to the raccoon sounded exactly like "axed." For these speakers, "Ask me!" comes out "Axe me!" I felt like a super fool when I realized that I transposed the **l** and **u** in superfluous, and in Sunday school, I invariably said "cavalry" instead of "Calvary." Even today I have to be careful not to transpose the **l** and the **v** of "relevant" and end

10

up with "revelant." Even trickier is keeping the **y** before the **n** in "larynx," and your efforts to achieve perfect pronunciation will be "foiled" if you put the **i** before the **l** in "foliage."

Obstacle 10: Letters with Multiple Sound Options

Vowels, diphthongs, and consonants are pronounced differently in different words.

Vowels

- The **a** in "made" is pronounced like the **ay** in "may."
- The **a** in "forbade" can be pronounced either like the **a** in "may" or like the **a** in "bad."
- The sound of the **a** in "father" is most often represented by the letter **o**—as in t**o**p, c**o**p, s**o**p, l**o**p, **o**pt—while an **a** in the same environment (t**a**p, c**a**p, s**a**p, l**a**p) has the sound of **a** in "apple."
- We have seen above that when an **a** ends a multisyllabic word in an unstressed syllable—as in "scub**a**," "tub**a**," and "moch**a**"—the **a** is invariably pronounced as a schwa: "scub**ə**," "tub**ə**," and "moch**ə**."
- The long **e** sound in "me" can also be represented as the **ee** of "ch**ee**se" and "sn**ee**ze," as **ei** as in "s**ei**ze," or as **ea** as in pl**ea**se and m**ea**t.
- On the other hand, **ea** in "great" has the sound of the **ay** in "may," but the **ea** in dead has the sound of **e** in "**E**d."
- But the **ea** in "measure" and "pleasure" can be pronounced as either the **ay** in "may" or as the **e** in "**E**d."

Diphthongs

Diphthongs are notorious for being unpredictable. The most inconsistent is **ou** and its variant **ow**.

11

- The **ou** of "Houston" rhymes with "**you**."
- The **ou** of "cough" sounds like the **au** in "caught."
- The **ou** of "bough" rhymes with "**cow**."
- The **ou** of "dough" rhymes with "**low**."
- The **ou** of "slough" sounds like "sl**ew**" when it means a swamp, but when it means to shed skin, the **ou** is pronounced as a schwa and the **gh** as **f**.
- The **ou** of "rough" is pronounced as a schwa and the **gh** as **f**.
- The **ou** of "nougat" always sounds like "sl**ew**."
- When "**row**" rhymes with "**cow**," it means a quarrel, but when "**row**" rhymes with "**low**," it means to use an oar.
- The **ou** of "route" has two acceptable pronunciations: one is the **oo** in "p**oo**l," and the other is the **ow** in "**cow**." But be sure to use the "p**oo**l" pronunciation when you're singing "Get Your Kicks on R**ou**te 66."

Consonants

- The **s** of "absurd" can be pronounced as either **s** or **z**, as can the **s** of "berserk."
- The **g** of "fungi" can be pronounced as the initial **g** in **g**iggle or like the **j** in **j**iggle.
- The final **g** in "garage" can be pronounced like the **g** in "bei**g**e" or like the **j** and **dg** in ju**dg**e.
- The first **c** in "circle" has a hissed **s** sound, while the second **c** has a **k** sound.
- And a host of different consonants and consonant combinations are pronounced **sh** in certain words, such as "**sh**irt," "**s**ure," "nation," "ocean," "**ch**ute," "**sch**wa," and "pre**c**ious."

12

Obstacle 11: Stress Can Be Erratic in English

Because of regional influences, some words can have primary stress on either of two syllables and still be pronounced correctly. For instance, either the first or the second syllable of "combatant" can be stressed: **COM**·ba·tant or com·**BAT**·ant. (Eastern Seaboard favors stressing the first syllable, while Midwestern Standard favors the latter pronunciation.) The same is true of "exquisite." Either the first syllable can be given the primary stress (**EX**·quis·itɘ) or the second (ex·**QUIS**·itɘ). With "disembark," either the first or last syllable can carry the primary stress (**DIS**·em·BARK or DIS·em·**BARK**).

Obstacle 12: Stress Switch Can Switch Meaning

Some words change their stressed syllable depending on their part of speech:

- When "frequent" is an adjective, the first syllable is stressed (**FRE**·quent): "We suffer from **FRE**·quent hurricanes." When "frequent" is a verb, the last syllable is stressed (fre·**QUENT**): "Which coffee shop do you fre·**QUENT**?"
- When "absent" is an adverb, the first syllable receives the primary stress (**AB**·sɘnt): "Why is Jim always **AB**·sɘnt?" When "absent" is a verb, the last syllable receives the primary stress (ab·**SENT** or ɘb·**SENT**): "Don't ab·**SENT** (or ɘb·**SENT**) yourself from Sunday school!"
- When "minute" is a noun meaning "a period of time," the primary stress is on the first syllable (**MIN**·it), which rhymes with "**spin** it." When "minute" is an adjective meaning "very small," the last syllable receives the primary stress (my·**NUTE**).
- When "perfect" is an adjective, it means "flawless" and the first syllable is stressed (**PER**·fect): "Rita speaks

13

PER·fect English." When "perfect" is a verb, it means "to make flawless" and the second syllable is stressed (per·FECT): "Tim is trying to per·FECT his English."

Did you notice that "perfect" in the title of this book can be read as an adjective (PER·fect pronunciation) or as a verb (per·FECT *your* pronunciation)?

Obstacle 13: Same Spelling—Different Sound and Meaning

Some words are spelled alike but change meaning depending on how one of the vowels is pronounced.

- When "isolate" is a verb meaning "to set apart," the **a** is pronounced like the long **a** in "ate": "Don't ɪ·sə·lāte yourself—it's party time!" When "isolate" is an adjective or a noun meaning "a person or thing that has become isolated," the **a** in **a**te becomes a short ĭ as in ĭt: "Basque has long been thought to be a language ɪ·sə·lit" (noun) or "Basque has long been thought to be an ɪ·sə·lit language" (adjective).
- When "dove" is a noun meaning "a kind of bird," its **o** has a schwa sound: "The Dəvᴇ left its calling card on my hat." When "dove" is a verb, the past tense of "to dive," its vowel is a long **o**: "Mr. America Dovᴇ off the Golden Gate Bridge."
- When "live" is a verb meaning "to exist," the **i** is short: "Where does the soul LIV?" When "live" is an adjective meaning "having life," the **i** is like the **ai** in **ai**sle: "The audience waited for the LAIV entertainment to begin."

Obstacle 14: Since When Is There an R in "Wash"?

In certain words, people add an extra sound (consonant, vowel, or semivowel sound), which linguists call *epenthetic sounds*. These epenthetic sounds may or may not be included as part of the proper spelling of the word. Epenthetic sounds can be classified as 1) unacceptable, 2) optional, or 3) absolutely essential to maintain the delicate interplay between voiced and devoiced consonants critical for clear communication.

Unacceptable Epenthetic Sounds

When I ask my students what their pet peeve in pronunciation is, near the top of their list is the epenthetic **r** their grandparents slip in before the **sh** of "wash" (wa**r**sh). Others complain about the extra **l** that speakers add after the **b** in "album" (alb**l**um). These mistakes never go unnoticed.

Additionally, an epenthetic **k** sound often sneaks in between the **e** and **s** of "escape" (e**k**scape). So in an academic or professional situation, don't let this epenthetic **k** escape your lips.

Other unacceptable epenthetic consonants are the **t** that some people attach to "across" (acros**t**), the **s** that some add to "anyway" (anyway**s**), and the **d** that some attach to the present tense of "drown" (drowne**d**). I was unaware that I was adding the **t** to "across" and the **d** to the end of "drown" until a friend pointed out my errors. I have since made a conscious effort to avoid these epenthetic consonants. To return the favor, I pointed out to my friend that he and his mother attached an epenthetic **l** to the end of "idea" (idea**l**). He made a conscious effort to continue adding the **l** to spite me for trying to correct him and his "MOMtionary."

Optional Epenthetic Sounds

The unwritten epenthetic semivowel **y** sound of "**y**es" is permitted, even preferred, in some words, especially of French origin, before **u** when **u** is pronounced like the **oo** in "pool." For example, the semivowel **y** sound is optional before the **u** of inure (in·**YOOR** or i·**NOOR**: to become accustomed to something painful or difficult). For another word of French origin, "legume," dictionaries only accept **LEG**·YOOM or li·**GYOOM**, both with an epenthetic **y** before

15

the **u.** However, when I asked my friend Bernie, a northern Illinois farmer, how he pronounced "L-E-G-U-M-E," he omitted the epenthetic **y** (**LEG·**OOM). Since he was my friend, I pointed out to him that *Webster* didn't permit his pronunciation, to which he replied, "I know an army of Midwesterners who pronounce it my way, and until someone can give a dadgum good reason for us to switch, we're sticking by our 'gumes." He has a point. If the dictionaries permit "inure" (i·**NOOR**) without an epenthetic **y**, they should also acknowledge Bernie's pronunciation of "legume" (**LEG·**OOM) as well as mine (le·**GOOM**).

An epenthetic semivowel **y** is also optional before the **u** in "Tuesday" (**TOOZ·**day or **TYOOZ·**day). Persons who choose the latter pronunciation often slip into **CHOOZ·**day, which is unacceptable to *Webster*. *Webster* does, however, allow us to "chew" the **tu** of **mature**, which can be pronounced as mə·**CHOOR**, mə·**TOOR**, or mə·**TYOOR**.

Essential Epenthetic Consonant and Vowel Sounds

An example of an epenthetic consonant that has sneaked into the language and has been accepted is the **b** in "number." Notice that there is no **b** in "numerous" or "numeral."

An example of a required epenthetic vowel is the schwa (ə) or short **ĭ** sound as in **ĭt**—both written as an **e**—that keeps pluralizing **s** from being absorbed by similar final consonant sounds called sibilants: voiceless **s** (**ss**), **sh**, **ch**, voiced **z** (**zz**), **zh** (the sound of **g** in bei**g**e), and **dz** (the sound of **j** and **dg** of **judge**).[5] Examples include "gases" (pronounced either as gasəz or gasĭz), "kisses" (kisəz or kisĭz), "brushes" (brushəz or brushĭz), "watches" (watchəz or watchĭz), "buzzes" (buzəz or buzĭz), "garages" (garazhəz or garazhĭz), and "judges" (judgəz or judgĭz).

---

[5] The basic rule is that only nouns that end in the voiceless consonant sounds **p**, **t**, and **k**, such as "co**p**," "be**t**," and "buc**k**," add a hissed pluralizing –s: "cops," "bets," and "bucks." In all other cases, you must buzz the pluralizing –s (or **es**). Therefore, "cobs," "beds," and "bugs" are pronounced "cob**z**," "bed**z**," and "bug**z**."

Exactly the same delicate interplay of voiced vs. voiceless consonants and epenthetic vowels that governed pluralization of the nouns from the earlier list applies to the formation of the third-person singular (the *she, he, it* form) of the present indicative verb tense:

- She "gas**es**" (pronounced as gasəz or gasĭz) up the car.
- He "kiss**es**" (kisəz or kisĭz) her feet.
- She "brush**es**" (brushəz or brushĭz) her hair.
- He "watch**es**" (watchəz or watchĭz) the clock.
- It "buzz**es**" (buzəz or buzĭz) in my ear.
- He says, "He 'garag**es**' (garazhəz or garazhĭz) the car."
- She "judg**es**" (judgəz or judgĭz) my actions.

The same epenthetic vowel sounds (schwa or short ĭ) that help form plurals and the third-person singular of verbs in the present indicative ending in sibilants[6] also apply when creating possessive adjectives. For instance, when you add **'s** to James (Jāmz) to form the possessive, as in "James**'s** house," you as a native speaker automatically add an epenthetic schwa or short ĭ sound to separate the sibilant sounds (Jāmz'əz or Jāmz'ĭz house). Even though you only add an apostrophe to the possessive of Jesus and Moses (Jesus' and Moses'), native speakers know to add an epenthetic schwa and an epenthetic **s.**

Obstacle 15: The Silencer—A Killer Virus

The interplay of voiced and voiceless consonants, the very backbone of the English language, is being destroyed by a devoicing virus that is silently sweeping through Standard American English like the plague. Since neither victim nor listener (affected or not) recognizes the symptoms of the virus, miscommunication becomes an almost daily occurrence, with

---

[6] Recall that the sibilants are voiceless **s** (**ss**), **sh**, and **ch**, or voiced **z** (**zz**), **zh** (the sound of **g** in bei**g**e), and **dz** (the sound of **j** and **dg** of ju**dg**e).

neither speaker nor listener understanding why. Persons with a strong case of the devoicing virus change all word-final voiced consonants into their voiceless counterparts. Near hopeless cases also devoice the same voiced consonants within words.

I'll explain the symptoms by providing real-life examples as well as a cure. In this way, both the vocabulary you already know and the vocabulary you are going to learn will be virus-free.

*For those who have the virus, voiced **th** goes to voiceless **th***

Every speaker of English—even if virus ridden—can pronounce the initial **th** of "**th**em," which is voiced and sounds like a bumblebee under a comforter or your phone on vibrate. The voiced **th**, according to the International Pronunciation Alphabet (IPA), is called "eth" and is represented by the symbol ð. While maintaining the voiced **th** sound, pronounce "eth" (eð). If your **th** still sounds like your phone on vibrate, you are virus-free. But if your **th** now sounds like a slow leak in a bicycle tire, you have the devoicing virus. You are pronouncing the voiceless **th** in **th**in, symbolized by the IPA as θ, the Greek letter "theta" (θeta).

I became aware of the devoicing virus some twenty-five years ago when I was trying to teach my Spanish students how to pronounce the Spanish **d** when it is between vowels, as in "na**d**a" (naða: nothing). I explained to the class that Spanish **d** in that position is always pronounced like a voiced **th** (ð), as in "wi**th**" (wið). When I had each student pronounce "naða," they all pronounced it with a voiceless **th** (θ—naθa). To solve the mystery, I asked them individually to pronounce "with" (wið). Again, all twenty-five students pronounced "with" using the devoiced **th** of thin (wiθ).

The same fate befell all other words ending in the voiced **th** (ð) sound, such as "tithe" (tið: to give a percent of your earnings), "lithe" (lið: limber), "blithe" (blið: happy), "writhe" (wrið: twist in agony), and "bequeath" (bequeað: to leave in one's will). To help

18

my students make the voiced **th** sound in "na**d**a," I created a jingle in English, with both the sound and the meaning of naða:

NADA *nothing*

Nah, the girl means **nothing** to me really.
Besides, I find her all too squat and
squeally.

By capturing the sound of the voiced **th** in naða with an English word that begins with a voiced **th** (**the**), I found that all the students could pronounce not only naða with ease, but they could also voice the **th** between vowels and in final position in English, as in wi**th**out, ti**the**, li**the**, bli**the**, wri**the**, and bequea**th**. This gave me the idea that jingles are a quick and easy way to teach pronunciation and to fight the devoicing virus.

Unfortunately, dictionaries are unwittingly contributing to the spread of the devoicing virus by including the devoiced pronunciation of "with" (wiθ) along with its traditional pronunciation (wið). The same fate has befallen "blithe" (blaið: happy).

For those who have the virus, voiced word-final –b becomes its voiceless counterpart –p

A few years ago, while I was dining with family and friends at Red Lobster, the devoicing virus created a most embarrassing moment for everyone. My wife ordered red snapper. I said, "I'll take a lobster." My son said, "I would like to take a crap." The waiter responded that the bathroom was right behind him but would he like to order before he went? One of our friends burst into gales of laughter, while her husband asked what was funny. She explained that my son meant to say "crab"; however, he pronounced the **b** as a **p**, thus changing his "**crab**" prematurely into "**crap**."

19

*For those who have the virus, final voiced –**d** becomes its voiceless counterpart –**t***

Recently, I was baffled twice in one day by individuals devoicing word-final –**d.** In the morning, I arrived at a favorite coffee shop and announced to the barista that I was ready for my morning coffee. "Do you want a 'bolt'?" she asked. I thought that perhaps she meant a shot of espresso to jumpstart the day. Or did she say "boat?" My eyes swept through the shop in search of clues to her meaning. When I spied a coffee urn labeled "bold," I realized that she had the devoicing virus, which caused her to devoice the final consonant –**d** of "bol**d**," resulting in "bol**t**."

That same afternoon, I went to the library and told the librarian I had come to pick up some books from interlibrary loan. She asked, "Do you have a library cart?" I responded that I was only picking up two books, so I wouldn't need a cart. She repeated her request: "Do you have a library cart?" But then she caught herself and changed "car**t**" to "car**d**," revealing that she was still capable of voicing the word final –**d** and proving that those with the virus still have a chance of recovery.

*For those who have the virus, final voiced –**g** changes to voiceless –**k***

You know you have the virus when your girlfriend "Ma**g**" is instantly transformed into your boyfriend "Mac**k**," your "mu**g**" turns to "muc**k**," your "fla**g**" gives you nothing but "flac**k**," and you "chu**ck**" your beer rather than "chu**g**" it.

*For those who have the virus, a final –**z** sound becomes a hissed –**s***

If you are a virus victim, your "little white lie**s**" turn into "little white li**ce**" and your "la**z**y" pronunciation suddenly becomes "la**c**y."

President Obama, in a speech on the budget, devoiced the final –z sound of peas (peaz), and I understood him to say either we would have to eat "our peace," "our piece," "our Ps," or the virus-ridden "our peas." Virus-ridden "peas" made the best sense. Not wanting to believe the president's language—which is recognized worldwide as a model for Standard American English pronunciation—could be tainted by the virus, I asked my linguistics teacher to listen to a replay. He confirmed that the president had indeed devoiced the final –z sound of "peas."

"Does this mean that English will have to become a tonal language like Chinese and assign a different tone to each word in a group of sound-a-likes?" I asked.

"Just as bad" was his reply. "We will have to use vowel length to distinguish a pair of sound-a-likes. A vowel sound before a voiced consonant, even though the consonant has been devoiced by the virus, is still longer than the same vowel before its voiceless counterpart. Therefore, the **ea** of the President's "p**ea**s" has a slightly longer **e** sound than the **ea** of 'p**ea**ce' and the **ie** of 'p**ie**ce.'"

The problem is English speakers have no experience distinguishing words that differ only in vowel length. If the word is pronounced out of context (in isolation), we are left clueless as to which word is intended.

The devoicing virus is also spreading to the **z** sound within words. In linguistics class on June 20, 2011, a student acknowledged that she pronounced the first **s** in "business" with a hissed **s** sound rather than with a **z** sound. It could be argued that her hissing the first **s** in "business" as "bi**s**nis" was a spelling pronunciation, except that she also devoices the **zz** of "bli**zz**ard" and ends up with "bli**ss**art." Admittedly, a "**blizz**ard" can become a "**bliss** art" if classes are cancelled.

For those who have the virus, final voiced –v becomes its voiceless counterpart –f

Erin, a waitress at a popular restaurant (where I am paid in coffee and milkshakes to help the English speakers with their grammar and pronunciation as well as to translate for the Spanish-speaking help), approached me and asked, "Professor, how do you pronounce this word: Is it 'mofe' or 'mauf'?" It was only after she wrote it down that I discovered the word in question was the color "mauve." There was not a trace of voicing in her final **v**.

To see how far her virus had spread, I asked her to pronounce "r-e-v-e-r-e-n-c-e." As I had feared, it came out as "reference," indicating that the virus was causing her to devoice both the final **v** and the **v** within words. As our conversation continued, I discovered that she was devoicing all final voiced consonants as well as those within words. For her, "sing" was pronounced "sink" and "singer" as "sinker." Additionally, she pronounced her favorite vegetable "corn on the co**b**" as "corn on the co**p**."

For those who have the virus, voiced –zh becomes its voiceless –sh counterpart

Because of the devoicing virus, the voiced **zh** sound represented by the **g** in "beige" and the **s** in "usual," "pleasure," and "measure" is rapidly facing extinction in not only word-final position but also within a word. I often joked that if devoicing ever reached the **zh** sound in word-initial position, every Jacques (ZHOCK) would be in for a real SHOCK. It turned out that I was the one who was in for the shock! At 9:06 this morning (December 29, 2011), I heard Liz, a twenty-five-year-old college student from Rochelle, IL, pronounce Jacques as SHOCK. To my utter dismay, I had actually found a person who has already completely lost an English sound through the devoicing virus! In other words, Liz represents the prototype of Standard American English

22

pronunciation in the very near future unless the devoicing virus is checked.

To test yourself for the devoicing virus, simply put a finger in each ear and pronounce the following pairs of words. The first column contains words ending in voiceless (devoiced or whispered) consonants, while the second has words that end in their voiced counterparts.

Devoiced final consonants	*Voiced final consonants*
p as in co**p**	**b** as in co**b**
t as in ba**t**	**d** as in ba**d**
k as in ba**ck**	**g** as in ba**g**
f as in re**f**	**v** as in re**v**
s as in bu**s**	**z** as in bu**zz**
sh as in bayi**sh**	**zh** as **g** in bei**g**e
ch as in mat**ch**	**dz** as in Ma**dg**e
th as in ba**th**	**th** as in ba**the**

If you are virus-free, you felt and heard your vocal cords vibrating the voiced final consonants, but if you have the virus, you didn't feel anything for either set of words. You only heard a whisper. Not to worry! For a quick self-cure (still with a finger in each ear), pronounce the following words. Pay close attention to what the initial voiced consonant sounds like and repeat the same sound for the final consonant.

Voiced initial and final consonants
b as in **bob**
d as in **dad**
g as in **gig**
v as in **Viv**
z as in [pi]**zazz**
dz as both **j** and **dg** in **judge**
zh as in **Zsa Zsa**
th as in **the th**[em]

Now you are able to "buzz like a bee" as well as "hiss like a snake," as Mohammad Ali might tell you to do.

Obstacle 16: When Simpler Isn't Better

There are core grammar and pronunciation rules that all speakers of English are expected to know. These rules are taught in the first years of elementary school and then promptly forgotten. Once speakers forget these rules, they make up their own simplified versions, a process linguists call *optimizing* the language. This tendency to simplify language diminishes a speaker's credibility in both social and professional situations. Your vocabulary can be extensive and your pronunciation perfect, but if you optimize (simplify) your language, you are but a mannequin dressed in silk.

Optimizing Pronouns: Me, Myself, and I

The most commonly forgotten rule is when to use subject and object pronouns and how to form and pronounce the reflexive pronouns.

Grammatical subjects and subject pronouns (I, you, he, she, it, we, you, they)
1)   do the action of action verbs:
      I ski   **we** love
      you [singular] drive   **you** [plural] dream
      she/he/it swims   **they** play

2)   stand on both sides of the verb "to be"
      I am the **teacher**. (**I** am **he**.)
      You are the **queen**. (**You** are **she**.)
      Bill is taller than **Jill** [is]. (**He** is taller than **she** [is].)
      If **I** were **Tim**, I wouldn't be such a jerk. (If **I** were **he**, I wouldn't be such a jerk.)

24

No adult native speaker of English ever makes the mistake of placing an object pronoun (me, him, her, us, them) before an action verb or before the verb "to be." Sentences such as "Me play Monopoly," "Him is my friend," "Us go to the store," and "Her swims in the lagoon" are considered to be pure baby-talk.

Yet when two subject pronouns precede an action verb (**He** and **I** fish), and when even a single subject pronoun follows the verb "to be" (It is **he**), optimizing the language sets in. Subject pronouns are converted to object pronouns as in baby-talk. My students invariably combine sentences such as "I play Monopoly" and "She plays Monopoly" into "Her and me play Monopoly." I have been waiting for half a century to overhear a college student utter "She and I" followed by an action verb.

Even the infallible TV detective Adrian Monk, in an unguarded moment, cried out, "It's him, it's him, it's him!" when he should have shouted, "It's he, it's he, it's he!" With every "him," his credibility went down, down, down!

President Obama, himself, is not immune to optimizing. When he was called on in an interview to make a statement about Congressman Wiener's shenanigans, he said, "If **I** was **him**, I would resign." The president had followed the verb "to be" with the object pronoun "him" instead of the correct "he."

Incorrectly, people are swayed into using object pronouns after the verb "to be" because they don't make a distinction between action verbs that are followed by object pronouns and "to be," which is not an action verb. Direct objects (DO) and their corresponding pronouns (DOP) receive the action of action verbs. Indirect objects (IO) and their corresponding pronouns (INDOP) receive the direct object:

George left his money [DO] to his cats [INDO].
He left it [DOP] to them [INDOP].[7]

---

[7] Even if you switch the word order to "George left his cats his money," "cats" remains the indirect object and "money" the direct object.

In the same breath in which the president optimized his pronoun ("If I was him"), he also optimized his verb choice by using "was," an indicative form of "to be," instead of "were," the required past subjunctive for a contrary-to-fact situation in the present (President Obama is not now and never will be Congressman Wiener). Optimizing the linguistic "game" of Indicative vs. Subjunctive verb use has become so pervasive that it is the focus of my next book.

Optimizing pronouns extends to the erosion of the spelling, use, and pronunciation of reflexive pronouns (myself, yourself, himself, etc.), which are meant to replace direct- or indirect-object pronouns that are the same as the subject of the sentence: "**I** see **myself** [direct object] in the mirror." "I gave **myself** [indirect object] the day off."

To see if you are an optimizer of reflexive pronouns, answer the following question with a single personal pronoun: When you and I look in the mirror, who do we see? We see _____.

If your answer is **us** ("We see **us**"), you have optimized personal pronouns by replacing the reflexive pronouns with object pronouns (me, you, him, her, it, us, you, them), exactly the pronouns that reflexive pronouns are supposed to replace when the subject of the sentence and the object are the same.

If you chose **ourselfs** ("We see **ourselfs**"), you have changed the voiced –v to its voiceless counterpart –f, ignoring the age-old rule in English that final **f** changes to a **v** when it is no longer in word-final position, as in the plural. Thus "sel**f**" becomes "sel**ves**" (**vz**), just as "leaf" becomes "leaves" (**vz**) and "knife" becomes "knives" (**vz**). Optimizers who ignore this rule are swayed by exceptions in which "chief" and "belief" maintain the **f** in the plural ("chie**fs**" and "belie**fs**"), and by listening to speakers with the devoicing virus that causes them to pronounce the final **vz** sound of "selves" (sel**vz**) as **fs**, resulting in "sel**fs**."

If you selected **ourself**, you have not only devoiced the **vz** sound of "ourselves," but you have also made **selves** singular—to parallel myself, yourself, herself, etc. If you optimize "ourselves," you probably also change plural "yourselves" to its singular form "yourself," eliminating the last distinction in the language between "you" singular and "you" plural.

If you answered <u>We see **ourselves**</u>, you should be congratulated, as you belong to a very select minority of speakers of Standard American English who neither devoice final voiced consonants nor optimize reflexive pronouns. The situation has become so bad that my computer recognizes **ourself** (the incorrect answer) as being acceptable and only questions the correct answer (**ourselves**).

Obstacle 17: Whose Pronunciation Not to Challenge

Eleven-year-old Paityn, the daughter of a friend, found out at an early age that you should never try to correct the pronunciation of a superior. When her fifth-grade teacher said, "Class, keep your eyes on me," it sounded to Paityn as though her teacher was saying, "Class, keep your 'ice' on me!" When she pointed out her observation to the teacher, she was told, "Young lady, don't ever try to correct my English!"

A few years ago, I attended a cocktail party in which a friend and colleague announced to the hostess that she really liked the "aged" (a·gəd) cheeses. The hostess gave her a questioning look and changed the subject. I then took my friend aside and pointed out that her cheeses and wines should be AGD and her men A·gəd. She hasn't spoken to this A·gəd man since.

Instead of trying to correct the pronunciation of a superior or friend, offer them a copy of *Perfect Pronunciation, By Jingle!*

Obstacle 18: Where Did All the Linguists Go?

There is no reason for English to be one of the most difficult languages to learn. English needs to implement a phonetic alphabet so our children can learn to read and write in a few days rather than struggle for a lifetime. It is the antiquated spelling system that makes mastery difficult. And to compound the problem, millions of English speakers have developed the devoicing virus that is causing a breakdown in communication.

Although linguists recognized the onset of the devoicing virus over fifty years ago, they have done nothing to alert parents and teachers to its existence and to the consequences if not checked. To linguists, language change is inevitable and nothing can be done to halt its natural evolution, even if the change hinders communication. Linguists pride themselves in being strictly *descriptivists* (those who document language change), but unfortunately, their descriptions are only written for and read by other linguists. Says one renowned linguist: "I don't set myself as an arbiter of fashionable speech."[8] The irony is that although the dozen or more linguists with whom I have studied all recognized that the language is changing, they insisted that phonetic transcriptions on their tests reflect Standard American English.

Now that the very fabric of the English sound system is being destroyed through the devoicing virus, linguists must come down from their ivory towers and help stem the tide.

---

[8] Peter Ladefoged, *A Course in Phonetics* (Chicago: Harcourt Brace Jovanovich, Inc., 1982), 83.

My Solution

A simple jingle proved to be the ideal vehicle for facing the challenge of correcting pronunciation. First, jingles can be written so they capture the natural stress pattern of the word to be learned. (Many, many mispronunciations result from a person stressing the wrong syllable of a word.) Second, jingles provide a context in which the word can be used. Third, people like to use jingles to remember facts. We learned to count with "One two buckle my shoe …" We recall the date of the arrival of the Spanish in America with the jingle, "In 1492, Columbus sailed the ocean blue …" We know the number of days in each month with the help of the jingle, "Thirty days hath September, April, June, and November …"

Jingles, too, have been used to help us remember pronunciation. To promote the correct pronunciation of "epitome," Willard R. Espy wrote the following verse:

E-PIT-o-me is kind and fair
Of evil EP-i-tome beware.
Of mispronunciation he
Is clearly the e-PIT-ome.[9]

---

[9] Willard R. Espy, *Say it My Way* (New York: Doubleday, 1980).

Charles Harrington Elster also wrote a jingle as a memory aid (mnemonic[10] device) to help us remember the pronunciation of "assuage" (to soothe):

All the world's a stage
And that's how you rhyme *assuage*.[11]

People would use jingles more often as memory pegs, but it often takes more time to make up a rhyme than to learn the fact by rote memory. I came to write *Perfect Pronunciation, By Jingle!* as a result of the success of my method in our *Portuguese Memory Book* and three Spanish memory books. This method is meant to replace the usual repeat-the-word-over-and-over-until-it-sticks method by expanding on a natural process of using the sounds of a familiar word or words to remember the sounds of a new word. However, the natural process produces mispronunciations if the sounds of a familiar word or words do not turn out to exactly match the sounds of the new word. For example, people mistakenly say "cold slaw" instead of "cole slaw" because they don't know what "cole" (a kind of cabbage) means and because "cole slaw" is served cold. To illustrate how my method works, consider the following example:

COLE   *a kind of cabbage*

Coal is always burned for heat,
Cole slaw's always good to eat.

As you can see, to help you remember the pronunciation of "cole," I took a familiar word (coal) with exactly the same sound and incorporated it in a jingle that also contains the unfamiliar word

---

[10] See the word "mnemonic" in the jingles for its pronunciation.

[11] Charles Harrington Elster, *The Big Book of Beastly Mispronunciation: The Complete Opinionated Guide for the Careful Speaker* (New York: Houghton Mifflin Co., 2005), 45.

(**cole**). To distinguish the key word from its sound-alike, I put the key word in bold (**cole**) and underscored its sound-alike (<u>coal</u>).

If we could find a familiar word sound-alike for every mispronounced word, learning pronunciation would be simple. But such matches are extremely limited. To increase the number of sound matches, I tried combining the sound of two or more familiar words that make the sound of a difficult one. For **centaur**, I found a two-word sound match in <u>sent or</u>.

CEN·taur *a mythical monster, part man and part horse*

You say mosquitoes love our <u>scent or</u>
  sound?
They think we're **centaur**s? I'll be bound!

Using two or three familiar words to teach the pronunciation of a difficult one more than doubles the possible sound matches, and people enjoy looking for multiple words that match the sound of a familiar one. Those who punish us with their puns often do so by playing with multiple words that sound just like a single word:

- "Extra police were called to the daycare center, where a number of the children had been resisting <u>a rest</u>."
- "What would you do if your nose went on strike? <u>Pick it</u>?"
- "You'll be stuck with that debt if you can't <u>budge it</u>."
- "How much does a pirate pay to have his ears pierced? A <u>buck an ear</u>."

But the number of two- and three-word matches is also limited. Then I discovered that just a *part* of a familiar word could be used to capture the pronunciation of a difficult or often-mispronounced one. For the sound of **czar**, there is the exact sound match in the **zar** of bi<u>zar</u>re.

31

CZAR   *ruler of Russia until 1917; one with great power*

—Isn't it quite bi<u>za</u>rre to live in trees?
—Not so, since I'm the **czar** of honeybees.

The addition of parts of familiar words to capture the sound of the key word increases the range of possible sound matches exponentially. A partial word can also be combined with a whole word to match the sound of a difficult word. <u>Dee</u> combined with the **po**– of <u>po</u>stponed (<u>dee po</u>) provides an exact sound match for **depot** with its silent "t."

DE·pot   *railway station*

<u>Dee po</u>stponed her wedding trip with pain:
Our little **depot** hasn't any train.

Two or more partial words can be combined to form the sound of a difficult one. The exact pronunciation of the key word **conundrum** (riddle) can be duplicated by combining the last (and unstressed) syllable of Dun<u>can</u> (cən) and the first two syllables of <u>undram</u>atically (əN·drəm).

co·**NUN·**drum   *a difficult riddle*

Dun<u>can undram</u>atically stated,
"I've solved our life **conundrum**:
We're mis-mated!"

Although this method was developed for Portuguese and Spanish vocabulary-building, I have been able to find sound matches for hundreds of commonly mispronounced words in English and inextricably tie their correct sounds to their meaning in jingles.

32

In *Perfect Pronunciation, By Jingle!*, I add several features. One of these is a caution when words contain an unexpected pitfall or have several acceptable pronunciations that you should know about. The caution is also expressed as a jingle and is found below the jingle containing the sound and meaning of the key word. Thus, the two jingles work together to make it easier for you to remember the pronunciation of the key word, as in the following example:

ARC·tic   *relating to the region around the North Pole*

After you <u>park, tick</u> off the silent hours.
Tell her her timid eyes are **Arctic** flowers.
In short, exert your best persuasive powers!

Caution!   *Two c's are in this word,*
So let them both be heard!

I have also added illustrations to make the context of some of the jingles more vivid. These have been provided by Sophia Varcados. Should you have some colored pencils handy, feel free to color the illustrations. In this way you will reinforce the memory tie between picture and jingle.

Conventions in this Book

1. Some of the jingles are purposely irreverent simply to make them easier to remember. Honestly, I would never cook a chameleon, kick a cat, or nuke a neighbor. You will find when you create your own jingles that they are easier to remember if they are out of the norm.

2. In the jingles, the indefinite article "**a**" is always in connected speech and therefore should be pronounced as schwa (like the **u** in "f**u**n"). In the jingles, the –**e** of the definite article "th**e**" should also always be pronounced as a schwa.

3. Each word is introduced with a definition. For the words with only one pronunciation, the word is broken into syllables showing the stress. Words with more than one acceptable dictionary pronunciation are introduced with the word in bold plus the number of possible pronunciations. I then either give a jingle for each pronunciation or tell you in a second jingle what sound changes are needed for the other pronunciations. Rather than trying to learn all the possible pronunciations of a word, choose the one with which you feel the most comfortable.

4. In the jingles, I always try to present the sound of the word to be learned before presenting the word itself. In a few cases, the sound is presented after the word.

5. If the jingle is a dialogue, a dash (—) introduces the speech of each speaker.

How to Use this Book

Each jingle in this book simultaneously provides you with the two most important pieces of information about an English word: its *sound* (pronunciation, including which syllable must be stressed) and its *sense* (meaning) in a natural setting. Illustrations are provided for over forty jingles to help you relate sound and sense. Often a caution (also in jingle form) is added to alert the reader to avoid a common error that people make in pronouncing the word.

The following jingle accompanied by an illustration and caution show how the method works. The word to be learned is **acme** (peak, pinnacle), with its stress on the first syllable (AC·) in caps and boldface. The meter in which the jingle is written (da **DA** da **DA** da **DA**) automatically places the stress on that syllable (a T<u>AC me</u> **IF** you **WILL**). The illustration depicts a bird on a mountain peak (the AC·me) challenging its enemies. You need not memorize an entire lyric. Just remember the significant parts: the bird on the mountain top and "Att<u>ack me</u> if you will." The caution warns that speakers often confuse "acme" (pinnacle) and "acne" (pimples).

acme

AC·me   *peak, pinnacle*

Att<u>ack me</u> for my judgments if you will.
I am the **acme** for right thinking still.

Caution!   *If you change the <u>m</u> to <u>n</u>*
*You'll get pimples (**acne**) then.*

When a word has more than one acceptable pronunciation, the number of possible acceptable pronunciations is indicated in parentheses after the initial word introduction (1), (2), etc. as in the following example:

cannabis (2)   *hemp: source of marijuana*

(1) CANN·a·bis   <u>Can a bus</u> convey without frustration
                      A load of truants smoking with elation
                      Cannabis and other vegetation?

(2) CANN·a·BIS   Smoke or not, you'll find your bliss
                      If you rhyme the **BIS** with k**iss**.

You choose the pronunciation that suits your fancy.

Since space does not permit an illustration for each jingle, conjure up an image that captures the sound and the sense of the word. For example, the image I like best for cannabis is a bus with smoke and music radiating out of its windows. Then I ask myself: <u>Can a bus</u> convey a load of truants smoking pot?

In words of one syllable (capital letters and bold), its vowel/diphthong automatically carries the primary stress (**RUN, A, CROP, I, MAIL, SHOUT, WOW**). **CREEK** illustrates this convention.

CREEK   *a stream, often a tributary to a river*

                 The atti<u>c reek</u>s of stale tobacco smoke.
                 The Rush **Creek** Gang meets here when broke.

Caution! *By any name, a creek*
            Perforce must rhyme with Greek.

With these strategies, you are ready to begin.

Perfect Pronunciation, By Jingle!

---

absent (2)   *a verb meaning "to keep (oneself) away"*

(1) AB·**SENT**   Ah<u>ab sent</u> a message calm and cool:
The boys must not **absent** themselves from
         school.
(Even if they only sit and drool.)

Caution!   *To make it clear just what you meant,*
*Put the stress upon the **SENT**.*

(2) ab·**SENT**   For this word you'll find a rub:
Ab can sound like **ub** in t**ub**.

---

a·**BYSS**   *an immeasurably deep pit*

<u>A</u>* <u>bis</u>cuit or a bun is all I need for supper.
The heady fumes from yon **abyss** will serve as
         picker-upper.

Caution!   *In this book, recall that "a" alone is always*
         uh
*(The same schwa sound you hear in "D**uh**!").*

AC·**CEDE**	*to express approval or consent*
	Look, Jack, see Dolores beat her breast Because you won't **accede** to her request.

AC·cu·rate	*free from error*
	—Jack, you're a terrible mathematician. —An **accurate** phrase to describe my division.

---

a·**CROSS**	*to or on the opposite side of*
	A* cross lay on the victim's breast. And "Satan" was scrawled **across** his chest.
Caution!	**Recall that "a" alone is always **uh** (The same schwa sound you hear in "**D**uh!").*
Caution!	*End this with a hissing **s**, Just as you do in saying "yes."*

---

adieu (2)	*farewell*
(1) a·**DIEU**	A dew of blood and tears has stained our garden. The die is cast. **Adieu** to peace and pardon.
(2) a·**DIEU**	Bud, you'll never make a Frenchman sore, If after **d**, you add the sound of **y** in **y**ore.

AD·mi·ra·ble   *causing wonder and respect*

Add myrrh,* a bull, and some gold—
An **admirable** gift, so I'm told.

Caution!   **Myrrh is like the **murr** in **Murray***
*Rhyming with the **furr** in **furry**.*

———————

adult (2)   *grown person*

(1) a·**DULT**   A dull tirade disturbed the monthly business
                          meeting
                   When most of the **adults** rose up demanding
                          central heating.

Caution!   *This is something not occult:*
*Most folks put the stress upon the **DULT**.*

(2) **AD**·ULT   Most things bad'll turn out good
                   When **adult**s do the things they should.

Caution!   *But here things will not turn out bad*
*If by chance you stress initial **ad**.*

40

aerie

aerie (4)   *the nest of a bird on a height*

(1) **AER**·ie   Getting an <u>airy</u> view of agriculture,
                          High in his **aerie** sits the watchful vulture.

(2) **AE**·rie   Getting an <u>eerie</u> view of agriculture,
                          High in his **aerie** sits the watchful vulture.

(3), (4)   There're two more ways to say this word,
                          But rhymes for them have not occurred.

Aesop (2)   *ancient Greek author of animal stories with morals*

(1) **AE**·SOP   Bee sopped up the messy chairs and tables
                 And cheered us by reciting **Aesop**'s Fables.

(2) **AE**·sop   She supposed we'd clean her stables
                 If she read us **Aesop**'s Fables.

———————

affluent (2)   *prosperous*

(1) **AFF**·luent   Her laugh flew untiringly into his dreams,
                 But her **affluent** father was onto his schemes.

(2) a·**FFLU**·ent   You won't commit a social gaffe
                 Putting stress on **fflu** or **aff**.

———————

aged (2)   *an adjective meaning "grown old"*

(1) **A**·ged   Her age adjusted to her made-up features,
                 Our **aged** Ms. attracts all kinds of creatures.

(2) **A**·GED   A careful speaker (likely not a kid)
                 Will choose to change the **ud** to **id**.

Caution!   *There are two syllables in this word.*
                 To make it one just sounds absurd,
                 Except for cheese and wine and curd.

| **AGED** | *past tense and past participle of the verb "to age"; allowed to grow old like wine and cheese* |
| | |

—Has Nemo's <u>age </u>destroyed his reason?
—True, he **aged** a lot this season.

Caution!   *Though just one syllable, this simple verb*
Says everything with brevity superb.

———————

agile (2)   *able to move quickly and easily*

(1) **AG**·ile   <u>Madge'll</u> find a surer way to win.
Her **agile** mind will even turn to sin.

(2) **AG**·ILE   <u>Madge, I'll</u> find a surer way to win.
My **agile** mind will even turn to sin.

———————

AG·o·ra   *marketplace in ancient Greek cities*

Bring me a <u>bag er a</u> bucket to hold
Botanical specimens dearer than gold.
They're bound for the **agora**, there to be sold.

Caution!   *By Grecian ghosts you won't be cursed*
For stressing syllable the first.

AG·or·a·**PHO**·bi·a   *a morbid fear of open spaces*

With ni<u>ageraphobia</u>, your fear is of falling.
With **agoraphobia**, open space is appalling.

Caution!   *We don't want to seem to nag,*
But put some stress upon the AG.

_____

AL·gae   *plural of alga (seaweed)*

<u>Al, gee</u> willikers—it really seems
Algae ends our fishing dreams.

_____

alias (2)   *assumed name*

(1) **A**·li·as   My <u>daily as</u>signment is ever the same:
Take a new **alias**, start a new game.

(2) **AL**·ias   The <u>ale ya s</u>lobber on the table
Decries your **alias**, "Clark Gable."

_____

alleged (2)   *so-called*

(1) al·**LEGED**   <u>Abel edged</u> slyly in through the door;
The **alleged** intruder lay drunk on the floor.

Caution!   *Just two syllables has this word.*
It's the version much preferred.

(2) al·**LEG**·ed   Should you make the syllables three,
You'll find you've joined the minority.

almond

almond (5)   *a kind of nut*

(1) **AL**·mond   T<u>om und</u>id his belt to make
More room for Thelma's **almond** cake.

(2) **AL**·mond   Delete the "l" or leave it in;
Either way you're sure to win.

(3), (4), (5)   There are three more ways to say this word.
Our rhymes for them, we fear, are absurd.

alternative	*one of several choices*

al·**TER**·na·tive

Why, D<u>oll, turn a Ti</u>voli into a sink of sin?
You've left me no **alternative**. I'll have to
turn you in.

Caution!

We have no choice of no or yes:
***Tur** alone must get the stress.*

---

amateur (4)

*one who engages in a pursuit as a pastime
rather than as a profession*

(1) **AM**·a·TEUR

<u>Sam, a chewer</u> of mundungus snuff,
Tops all **amateur**s at spitting the stuff.

(2) **AM**·a·teur

Make this word your double feature:
Rhyme the **teur** with **cher** of tea**cher**.

(3) **AM**·a·TEUR

<u>Sam, a tour</u> de force is badly needed
For **amateur**s, like we, to be top-seeded.

(4) **AM**·a·teur

<u>Sam, a terrific</u> inventor of jests
Plays **amateur** clown to occasional guests.

Caution!

*Rhyme the **teur**
With "Thank you, **sir**."*

amphetamine (2)   *a compound used in sprays for head colds*

(1) am·**PHET**·a·MINE   They found the whole d<u>amn fête</u>* <u>a</u>
                             <u>means</u>
                  Of selling us **amphetamine**s.

   Caution!   **We may well disapprove but not*
                           debate:
                  In speaking English, we of course say
                        "fate."
                  But here, since rules for rhyming must
                        be met,
                  We've used the French pronunciation,
                        "fett."

(2) am·**PHET**·a·mine   You'll find it's not a mortal sin
                  To also sound the **mean** as **min**.
                  But if you do, we must confess,
                  You'll need to strip it of its stress.

———————

AM·pho·ra   *ancient Greek jar*

                  I don't give a d<u>amn fer a</u> classical bust,
                  But I'll drink from her **amphora**, seein' I
                      must.

———————

ancient (2)   *relating to a time early in history*

(1) **AN**·cient   <u>Jane, shun t</u>ricks of TV advertisers
             Who play the **ancient** role of health advisers.

(2) **AN**·cient   Not to leave you in the lurch,
             C can sound like **ch** in **ch**urch.

anon

a·**NON**   *immediately, soon, shortly*

A nondescript letter arrived in the mail.
Anon, the ump hoped it was written in
    Braille.

Antarctic

ant·**ARC**·tic   *relating to the region around the South Pole*

Aunt, Arctic winds delay you from your plan
Of seeking **Antarctic** regions perilous to man.

Caution!   **Antarctic**, *like Arctic, contains two* **c**'s.
Pronounce each one of them clearly, please!

antennae (2)   *plural of antenna (an organ of sensation on the heads of insects)*

(1) an·**TENN**·ae   Can ten ecologists resolve my doubt,
                          Why butterflies' **antennae** don't fall out?

 (2) an·**TENN**·as   Science makes this plural with **e**.
                          Common folks add **s** like me.

ANY·WAY   *in any case*

                          "**Anyway**," said Bonnie, looking regal,
                          "Any waiver is considered legal
                          If you stamp it with the U.S. eagle!"

Caution!   *Please don't be a common jay*
                          *By adding **s** to "anyway."*

----

aqueous (2)   *watery*

(1) **A**·que·ous   The skin-divers ache, we assume, to explore
                          The **aqueous** world of the ocean floor.

(2) **AQ**·ue·ous   Change **ache** to **ak**,
                          You'll get no flack.

ARC·tic   *relating to the region around the North Pole*

After you <u>park, tick</u> off the silent hours.
Tell her her timid eyes are **Arctic** flowers.
In short, exert your best persuasive powers!

Caution!   *Two **c**'s are in this word.*
So let them both be heard!

———————

AR·gent   *silvery*

Where is my <u>large, unt</u>iring sergeant?
The stars are bright, the moon is **argent**!

argot

argot (2)   *slang; specialized vocabulary used by those in the same type of work*

(1) **AR**·GOT   You let my <u>car go</u> straight to hell!
(To use the **argot** that you know so well.)

(2) **AR**·GOT   The French won't want to hear it—but
You can also change the **go** to **gut**.

———————

aria (2)   *a solo in a classical opera*

(1) **AR**·i·a   I'm <u>sorry a</u> sneeze escaped my nose
Before the **aria**'s moving close.

(2) **A**·ri·a   —There's an opera in the <u>area</u>, isn't it so?
—No, the **aria**'s in the opera, didn't you
know?

arthritis (2)   *an inflammation of the joints*

(1) ar·**THRI**·tis   —I'm sure you could, <u>Arth, write us</u> Chinese
                                           books
                                  And reproduce those graceful lines and hooks.
                                  —**Arthritis** makes it harder than it looks.

(2) ar·**THRI**·tis   In careful speech, you'll be in bliss
                                  If you'll rhyme **i-s** with **k**i**ss**.

Caution!   *Be careful here as you know how to be:*
                         Arthritis's syllables are only three.

————————

ASKED   past tense of *to inquire, request*

                         When I saw that the mugger was armed
                                  and m<u>asked,</u>
                         I swore that I'd do whatever he **asked**.

Caution!   *When this useful word you say,*
                         Put the **s** *before the* **k**.

————————

ASTH·ma   *a chronic lung disorder characterized by*
                             coughing, wheezing, and difficulty in
                             breathing

                            <u>As Ma</u> has **asthma**, she must always stay
                            Inside the house when we go out to play.

53

ath·**LET**·ics

*exercises, sports, or games engaged in by
athletes*

<u>C<u>ath</u>, let ex</u>citing tales about **athletics** and its
    heroes
Make you forget your hometown team: its
    scores are mostly zeroes.

Caution!

*Heed this caution. Try to learn it well.
Add no schwa between the **h** and **l**.*

---

attaché

ATT·a·**CHÉ**

*a technical expert on a diplomatic staff
stationed abroad*

<u>At a sha</u>dy rendezvous for spies,
The **attaché** displayed his new disguise.

54

| au·**GE**·an | *an adjective meaning "indescribably filthy like the stables of King Augeus, cleaned out by Hercules"* |

<u>Aw, gee! an</u> axe we'll need to cut the gloom
From that **Augean** stable—Ernie's room.

| **autopsy (2)** | *postmortem examination* |

(1) **AU**·TOP·sy

<u>Paw, Topsy</u> said you were hit on the head.
The **autopsy** showed that you really weren't
    dead.

(2) **AUT**·op·sy

Webster says—we dare not disagree—
It's also heard as <u>OUGHT up see</u>.

| **AWK**·ward | *clumsy, lacking dexterity* |

"<u>Awk! Word</u>s fail me," cackled my red hen.
"That **awkward** rooster cracked my eggs
    again!"

| **BILK** | *to cheat* |

The <u>bill c</u>ollectors call each week to scatter
    strife and gloom.
I hold my tongue and ask myself, "Just who is
    bilking whom?"

bi·ZARRE　　　　*odd, extravagant, or eccentric in style or mode*

The show-biz arguments are these:
We try to move, we try to please,
We teach about the birds and bees,
Show politicians on their knees,
Instruct you how to deal with fleas—
And do you think it so **bizarre**
We tell you where the bargains are?

———————

BON MOT　　　　*witty remark*

—The bone Moe wants to pick with you
Concerns your **bon mot** re: his stew.
—What I said I have no clue,
But it, like he, is hard to chew.

bouillon

bouillon (3)   *a clear, seasoned soup, usually from beef*

(1) **BOUILL**·on   This <u>bull yon</u> cow pursues with tender glances
                         Was born and raised for **bouillon**, not
                                   romances.

(2) **BOUILL**·on   If you change the **yon** to **yən**,
                         Just the French will come undone.

     French   The French will take you as their own
                         If you pronounce this word BOO·**YOWN**.

57

BROCC·o·li   *a vegetable resembling cauliflower*

If <u>Brock'll lea</u>ve the food to us
My **broccoli** salad's no real fuss.

Caution!   *Unlike a president we know,*
One must sound and schwa the second o.

———————

cadre (4)   *a military or training group*

(1) **CAD**·re   The <u>cad reg</u>rets his latest social error.
His **cadre** mates consider him a terror.

(2) **CA**·dre   The <u>cod Ray</u> caught to serve at dinner
Were so small we called him "winner."
(The **cadre** wants us all much thinner.)

(3) **CA**·dre   They say that <u>cod run</u> 'round in schools
Because their **cadre** teaches them rules
(And censure those who act like fools).

(4) **CA**·dre   <u>Cod, re</u>nowned for liver oil,
Makes the **cadre** all recoil.

cajole

ca·**JOLE**   *to dissuade with deliberate flattery*

The In<u>ca, Joel</u>, **cajole**d me into dancing
A step that's not allowed at home in Lansing.

cannabis (2)   *hemp: source of marijuana*

(1) **CANN**·a·bis   <u>Can a bus</u> convey without frustration
                         A load of truants smoking with elation
                         Cannabis and other vegetation?

(2) **CANN**·a·**BIS**   Smoke or not, you'll find your bliss
                         If you rhyme the **BIS** with k**iss**.

_____

CAN·o·py   *an awning or other covering fastened above a*
                         person, bed, throne, etc.

                         A **canopy** of stars illumed our treats—
                         A <u>can o' peas</u>, some leeks, and pickled beets.

Caution!   *Don't pronounce the **o'** in "can o' peas" as **o***
                                 *in g**o**.*
                         *It's short for **o** in "**of**"—a fact you surely*
                                 know.

_____

CAN·ta·**LOUPE**   *a kind of melon*

                         Those poor insects <u>can't elope</u>;
                         She's imprisoned in a **cantaloupe**.

Caution!   *When you say "elope" at rapid speed,*
                         *Initial **e** becomes the schwa we need.*

60

carafe (2)	*a bottle with a flaring lip used to hold beverages*
(1) ca·**RAFE**	My men, the an<u>chor af</u>ter all held fast. We'll drink a tall **carafe** to dangers past.
Caution!	***Chor** of an**chor**'s just like **cur**. Saying **core** will make me grrr.*
(2) ca·**RAFE**	Just as easy as to cough Is to change the **af** to **off**.

CEN·sor	*a person who examines written or pictured material and removes anything considered unsuitable*
	<u>Sense er</u> nonsense, students, it's the rule: The **censor** reads your mail at boarding school.

CEN·sure	*to condemn as wrong*
	We <u>sense you're</u> full of vim and vigor, But **censure** your religious rigor.

centaur

CEN·TAUR   *a mythical monster, part man and part horse*

You say mosquitoes love our <u>scent or</u> sound?
They think we're **centaur**s? I'll be bound!

chameleon

chameleon (2)   *a lizard that can change the color of its skin*

(1) cha·**MEL**·eon   Coo<u>k a mealy young</u> **chameleon** right within
                                      your stew.
                         Watch its golden spots and flecks take on an
                                        amber hue.

Caution!   *This word is Greek. That's why we say—*
                         *c-h must have the sound of **k**.*

(2) cha·**ME**·le·on   Coo<u>k a meal ya n</u>ever cooked before;
                         Like a **chameleon**, vary your décor;
                         Devise a gag to make the neighbors roar;
                         Buy a gown your husband will adore;
                         And then perhaps ya won't be such a bore.

CHAM·ois   *a small antelope of Europe and Asia prized for its soft skin*

Your <u>sham E</u>laine has caused a din,
You shot a **chamois** just for skin.
To save your soul from mortal sin,
You served its meat to all your kin.

———————

champion

CHAM·pi·on   *a first-place winner in a competition*

The <u>champ, 'e u</u>nexpectedly picked up the
    lightweight title,
Took punches in a dozen places, some of
    which were vital.
But how could such a **champion** go to sleep
    at my recital?

CHA·OS   *total confusion*

<u>Kay, ah!</u> scars on neck and lip
Speak of **chaos** on your trip.

Caution!   *Another word we get from Greek.*
"Chameleon" gives the sound we seek.

---

cha·RADE   *a game in which a word or phrase is acted out*
and the audience tries to guess it

Each week or two there comes a har<u>sher raid</u>.
There's talk of peace—but it's a mere
charade.

Caution!   *Indeed it gives us quite a wrench*
To find c-h spells sh in French.

---

cha·RIS·ma   *personal magic or leadership*

Tell me, Os<u>car, is M</u>atilda ready?
Make her hold her famed **charisma** steady.

Caution!   *This word's not French. It's Greek!*
So car not char is what we seek.

CHAR·la·tan   *a pretender to knowledge or ability*

<u>Charlotte un</u>covered the clergyman's crime.
He stole the fold's money, every last dime!
That **charlatan** soon will be doing his time.

65

CHIC   *currently fashionable*

I planned to wed a <u>sheikh</u> on finding
Such unions are both **chic** and binding.

———————

clan·**DES**·tine   *conducted with secrecy*

Arise, <u>clan destine</u>d to an ancient throne!
Clandestine raids will give you back your
        own.

———————

cli·**CHÉ**   *a trite expression*

Do ma<u>ke Lee sha</u>ke us up another drink
Before his bland **cliché**s begin to stink.

———————

clique (2)   *small, exclusive group of persons*

(1) **CLIQUE**   Take <u>leeks</u> and chop them extra fine,
Douse them in a pungent wine,
And all your **clique** will come to dine.

(2) **CLIQUE**   Our love could really <u>click</u> and quick
If you'd just drop your snobbish **clique**.

66

co·**HAB**·it   *to live with*

The co<u>coa habit,</u> addicts averred,
Cohabits with the wise and witty word.

Caution!   *Should you voice the **a** in cocoa,*
Folks will think you're really loco.

CO·HORT   *one tenth of a Roman legion, 300-600 men;*
figuratively, it came to refer to a group of
associates, and currently to a single associate
or colleague

<u>Coe, Horte</u>ncia hurt her hand
Shaking with her **cohort** band.

coiffure

COI·**FFURE**   *hairstyle*

You <u>quaff YOUR</u> home brew and I'll quaff
          MINE.
Like our **coiffures**, both versions are divine.

Caution!   *Here quaff must rhyme with **waff** of **waff**le*
*As well as with the **af** in fal**af**el.*

COLO·nel

a military officer ranking above a lieutenant colonel and below a brigadier general

Colonel, here's the <u>kernel</u> of the matter:
You're just a bit too fat and getting fatter.

Caution!

No wonder all the grade-school kids are yelling.
The sound has small connection with the spelling.

———————

CO·ma

unconsciousness usually due to disease or injury

The honey<u>comb a</u>dorns the maple tree,
A noontide **coma** lies on every bee,
The perfect place for drones like me.

Caution!

We make the point with some elation:
A coma's not for punctuation.

———————

conch (2)

a large spiral univalve shell

(1) CONCH

The <u>conq</u>uered insurgents lining the beach
We'd <u>conk</u>ed with **conch**s; a <u>conk</u> for each.

(2) CONCH

You can do whatever you please!
C-H, too, can sound like **ch** in **ch**eese.

conundrum

co·**NUN**·drum   *a difficult riddle*

Dun<u>can</u> <u>undram</u>atically stated,
"I've solved our life **conundrum**: We're
    mis-mated!"

Caution!   *Conundrum's just a fancy name for riddle.*
Like, "How's a hungry fellow like a fiddle?"
Answer: "He has a hollow in the middle."

COUP   *a sudden, successful move or action*

When Nemo taught his rooster how to <u>coo</u>,
His neighbors claimed he'd engineered a
coup.

coupon (2)	*a ticket enabling one to obtain an article or service at a reduced cost*
(1) **COU**·PON	Here's the s<u>coop on</u> Ernie's brand new truck. He got it for a **coupon** that he'd seen by luck.
Caution!	*Why does **O-U** sound like **oo** in **loo**p?* *It comes from French, and that's the poop.*
(2) **COU**·PON	*Webster's* says—we must obey— **Cue** for **coo**'s another way.

———————

courtier (2)	*one who practices flattery; an attendant at a royal court*
(1) **COURT**·ier	<u>Court</u> <u>yer</u> girl with gifts and kisses. A zealous **courtier** seldom misses.
(2) **COURT**·i·er	Between the **court** and **yer**, let out the **ee** of **ee**k, And you'll have made the very sound we seek.

———————

covert (2)	*secret*
(1) **COV**·ert	Bring the <u>cover</u>—torn, but soft and warm— For **covert** operations in the dorm.
(2) **CO**·vert	In the Corn Belt, think it over, The **O** should sound like **o** in D**o**ver.

crayon (2)	*a stick of colored wax for writing or drawing*

(1) **CRAY**·ON   Says little <u>Kray on</u> **crayon** coloring books,
                  "To stay within the lines is harder than it
                      looks."

(2) **CRAY**·on   A second way that we can't shun
                  Is unstressed **on** (sounds just like **un**).

CREEK   *a stream, often a tributary to a river*

The att<u>ic reek</u>s of stale tobacco smoke.
The Rush **Creek** Gang meets here when
    broke.

Caution!   *By any name, a **creek**
*Perforce must rhyme with **Greek**.*

CZAR   *ruler of Russia until 1917; one with great
power*

—Isn't it quite bi<u>zar</u>re to live in trees?
—Not so, since I'm the **czar** of honeybees.

Caution!   *I give you my best judgment on it:
The bees are in this fellow's bonnet.*

data (2)   *facts used as a basis, especially for discussion or decision*

(1) **DAT**·a   My <u>date a</u>roused the greatest rage
                             By asking **data** on my age.

(2) **DAT**·a   A second way (it's not too late):
                             Just put a **dat** in place of **date**.

_____

début (3)   *a formal entrance into society*

(1) **DÉ**·BUT   The <u>day beau</u>ticians finished Alice,
                             She made her **début** at the palace
                             But found the monarch cold and callous.

(2) DÉ·**BUT**   Above we stress initial **day**.
                             Stressing **beau-**'s the other way.

(3) dé·**BUT**   If you take all stress from **day**,
                             It's, well, **duh**! That's what you say.

Degas

Degas (2)   *French impressionist painter 1834-1917*

(1) De·**GAS**   After the earthquake, Sam <u>dug o</u>bjects from
the earth
To which **Degas**'s own hand might well have
given birth.

(2) DE·**GAS**   To say this name another way,
Simply rhyme **D-E** with **day**.

demur (2)   *to object to*

(1) DE·**MUR**   Dee<u>dee, mur</u>murs fill the summer air
Of organ music, hymns, and prayer.
I won't **demur**. (I do not dare.)

(2) DE·**MUR**   A second way, and here's the trick:
Just change the **dee** to **di** in **Di**ck.

Caution!   *With **U-R** here, you must be sure*
***Not** to have it sound like **your**.*

———————

DE·**MURE**   *affectedly modest or sedate*

Kim, you just fed <u>Dee mur</u>iatic acid!
And still you sit there so **demure** and placid.

Caution!   *With **U-R** here, you must be sure*
*Its very sound is that of **your**.*

———————

deter (2)   *to discourage or prevent from acting*

(1) de·**TER**   Dee<u>dee, turn</u> your eyes upon your childhood
      dreams.
They must **deter** you from all these wicked
      schemes.

(2) DE·**TER**   You'll master (2) so nice and quick
By changing **dee** to **di** in **Di**ck.

detour (2)   *go in a roundabout way*

(1) DE·TOUR   —Did <u>Dee tour</u> all the plains in Spain?
     —She had to **detour**—too much rain!

(2) DE·TOUR   Put the stress on **DE** or **TOUR**—
     Either way, you can be sure!

DID·n't   *contraction of "did not"*

Yes, I <u>did unt</u>ie your shoe.
But, oh! I swear I **didn't** do
Some other things I wanted to.
So won't you let me sit by you?

DOC·tor·al   *of a doctor*

We <u>docked Earl</u>'s boat and found him still
     alive.
His **doctoral** know-how helped the man
     survive.

DOGE   *chief magistrate in the former republics of Venice and Genoa*

The <u>dough J</u>im won on this day's crooked
     ballot
Is rich enough to tempt a **doge**'s palate.

ECH·e·LON   *any of the subdivisions in an organization*

M<u>esh a Long</u>ine watch or two with
      compliments and quips,
And dames in higher **echelons** will take you
      off on trips.

Caution!   *Longine watches were the rage
When I started on this page.*

———————

EE·rie   *frightening because of strangeness or
gloominess*

When chewing c<u>ere</u>al flake by flake,
Oh! What **eerie** sounds you make.

———————

EI·ther   *one or the other of two*

B<u>e the r</u>ealist you claim to be:
Either clench your fist or bend your knee.

British   There in England, Brits seem blither—
Rhyming "either" with their "Aye there!"

———————

e·LIX·ir   *a substance for transmuting metals into gold
or for prolonging life indefinitely*

After every meal J<u>ill licks</u> 'er luscious fingers,
Whereupon the scent of rare **elixir** lingers.

ennui (2)   *boredom*

(1) ENN·**UI**   D<u>on, we</u> don't feel **ennui** like other folks.
                        When we get bored, we just exchange stale
                            jokes.

(2) **ENN**·UI   You stress the **on** and not the **we**?
                        Not one of us will disagree.

---

ensign (2)   *a low-ranking naval officer*

(1) **EN**·SIGN   The m<u>en sin</u> daily, yet remain completely
                            charming.
                        Even **Ensign** Nora finds her shipmates quite
                            disarming.

(2) **EN**·sign   One more thing and then you're done:
                        Sin's okay, but so is **son**.

epitaph

EP·i·TAPH

an inscription on a tomb or a written tribute to a dead person

"Our Jill—with pep—would pr<u>ep a taffy</u>-pull."
(Her **epitaph** bespeaks a heart that's full.)

epitome

epitome (3)   *embodiment of a typical quality*

(1) e·**PIT**·o·ME   The <u>pit! Uh me!</u> you've fallen in! Confess—
You're the **epitome** of awkwardness.

(2) e·**PIT**·o·ME   If you're careful as can be,
The first **e** sounds like **e** in m**e**.

(3) e·**PIT**·o·ME   Or you have the choice to use
The **i** in **i**ck to suit your muse.

era (2)   *a period of time marked by some important event*

(1) **ER**·a   A baseball card of Yogi B<u>erra</u>
                      Marked for me the postwar **era**.

(2) **E**·ra   The sh<u>eer</u> appeal of sirloin steak and
                              scrambled eggs and butter
                      All through that **era** made me work and kept
                              me from the gutter.

                      ——————

ere

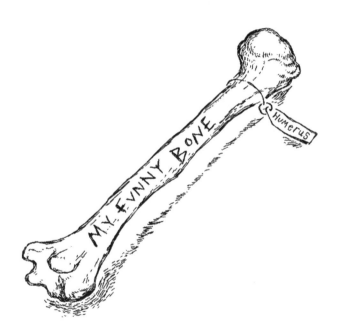

ERE   *before*

                      I want to <u>air</u> a last request:
                      Ere my bones are laid to rest
                      Inscribe them with a simple jest.

82

escape (3)   *a getting free*

(1) E·**SCAPE**   Y<u>es, cape</u>s for men today are all the rage.
It's our **escape** to the Romantic Age.

(2) E·**SCAPE**   Though we never like to pick,
Initial **e** can sound like **i** of **i**ck!

(3) e·**SCAPE**   Even schwa will do the trick.

Caution!   *Careful speakers all agree*
*There's no **k** before the **c**.*

---

es·**CHEW**   *to avoid, shun*

B<u>ess, chew</u> your nails and tear your hair,
But please **eschew** long underwear!

Caution!   *A caution you might guess:*
*Please don't eschew the **s**!*

British   Just the Brits—not me and you—
Change **C-H** to **sh** in **sh**oe!

---

es·**PRIT**   *vivacious wit or cleverness*

B<u>ess, pree</u>n yourself before the mirror.
Your famed **esprit** just makes it clearer
You're vainer every day—but dearer.

Caution!   *Silent **t**. The French, who should know better,*
Oftentimes delete the sound but not the letter.

83

exquisite (2)   *marked by flawless craftsmanship or beautiful execution*

(1) **EX**·quis·ite   A s<u>ex quiz I</u>talians presented with gusto and
                                       gravity
                   People now say is an **exquisite** work of
                                       depravity.

   Caution!   *Well begun—back East—is halfway done:*
                   So there they accent syllable number one.

(2) ex·**QUIS**·ite   When you put the stress on **quiz**,
                   In the Corn Belt, you're the whiz!

---

ex·**TOL**   *to praise highly*

                   <u>Rex, toll</u> the bell, and bow with grief.
                   Extol her life so blithe and brief.

   Caution!   *Three more ways to say this word*
                   In the Midwest just aren't heard.

extraordinary

ex·**TRAORD**·in·AR·y   *very unusual*

The unicorns <u>next roared in airy</u> cages.
Their keepers get **extraordinary**
        wages
For keeping myths alive throughout the
        ages.

Caution!   *This rule into my head was pounded:*
        *The **a** of extra isn't sounded.*

British   The Brits outdo us, and by far,
        Deleting **i** of **in** and **a** of **ar**.

FAUX PAS   *an error in etiquette*

—Your worst <u>foe—Pa</u>—has left and slammed
     the door.
—Her great **faux pas** is this: she's such a
     bore.

Caution!   *It's French, you see, and when you know*
     those people better,
You'll find, in many words, they hate to sound
     the final letter.

———————

FEB·ru·**AR**·y   *the second month*

A<u>lfeb, rue airy</u> promises you made,
If not—by **February** I'm afraid
Your valentines won't make the grade.

———————

FE·cal   *relating to bodily waste*

His <u>fee col</u>lected, Doctor Hatter
Sat down to deal with **fecal** matter.

FETT·le   *sound mental or physical shape*

The tourney and <u>féte'll</u>* put knights on their
        mettle,
And all the survivors will leave in fine **fettle**.

Caution!   **We may well disapprove, but not debate:*
In speaking English, we of course say "fate."
But here, since rules for rhyming must be met
We've used the French pronunciation "fett."

———————

flaccid (2)   *flabby, limp*

(1) **FLAC**·cid   The <u>flack Sid</u> passed among the boys is this:
Your **flaccid** lips have long forgot to kiss.

(2) **FLAC**·cid   *Webster* says it's quite okay
If you choose to mute **c-k**.

———————

FLOUT   *to scorn*

I<u>f lout</u>s like you are free to run our city,
Our crime statistics will be less than pretty!
You **flout** the laws of justice and of pity.

———————

forbade (2)   *past tense of forbid, prohibited*

(1) FOR·**BADE**   <u>Four bad</u> and angry men **forbade**
That I shoot out what brains you had.

(2) for·**BADE**   When first I learned, I was dismayed
That **bade** can also rhyme with m**ade**.

87

FOR·eign   *situated outside a place or country*

Be<u>fore un</u>chartcd **foreign** seas I sail,
I fear you'll have to get me out on bail.

---

forte (2)   *strong point*

(1) **FORT**·e   Nemo came to call with <u>four</u>teen bears.
They ate up all my rugs and half the chairs.
His **forte** must be promoting home repairs.

   Caution!   *Tell yourself both loud and clear:*
*The final **e** is silent here.*

(2) **FOR**·te   But if you slip and add an **ay**,
Stress the **FOR** and not the **tay**.

88

fracas

FRA·cas   *a noisy quarrel*

> —Let's join the verbal <u>fray, cuss</u> out those
>   nerds!
> —I fear this **fracas** can't be won by words.

———————

fre·**QUENT** (v.)   *to visit (a place) often*

> <u>Free Quent</u>in from his futile urge to think,
> And get him to **frequent** a trusty shrink.

FRE·quent (adj.)   *happening at short intervals, often*

That <u>freak went</u> out to **frequent** brunches,
Brought paper napkins home in bunches,
And used them for his homemade lunches.

FUCH·sia   *a vivid, reddish purple*

<u>Few shun</u> **fuchsia** underclothes,
Though they hamper deep repose.

FUGUE   *a musical composition governed by strict laws of counterpoint*

A <u>few g</u>reat names make human history
     glisten.
One plays a **fugue**; a thousand learn to listen.

---

fungi (2)   *plural of fungus, such as mushrooms or mold*

(1) **FUN**·gi   What <u>fun Guy</u> is! Though everybody knows
The guy has **fungi** in between his toes.

(2) **FUN**·gi   What <u>fun Giles</u> is! Though everybody knows
The guy has **fungi** in between his toes.

Caution!   *Say the **g** like **g** in **g**iggle*
*Okay, too, is **j** in **j**iggle.*

90

FUT·ile   *serving no useful purpose*

The clear re<u>fute'll</u> be all mine
Until your **futile** case evolves a spine.

British   The way to get a Brit to smile
Is say this word just like <u>few tile</u>.

GAFFE   *a social blunder*

Hedwi<u>g, aff</u>luent as she is (or seems),
Just made a **gaffe**: she told her wildest
      dreams.

---

gala (3)   *n. festival; adj. festive*

(1) **GA**·la   <u>Gay, La</u>Donna loved a ball.
Gala big or **gala** small,
She would dance in any hall.

(2) **GAL**·a   My <u>gal </u>awoke me drifting out to sea.
The **gala** ball had been too much for me.

(3) **GA**·la   While you're waltzing with your Dolly—
G-A also rhymes with **go** in **Go**lly.

genuine

GEN·u·ine   *really being what it is said to be*

                      <u>JEN, you in</u> a fit of cleaning up
                      Threw out my **genuine** Olympic cup.

---

ge·**STA·**tion   *conception and development, especially in the*
                      mind

                      <u>Jess, stationed</u> at the nearest exit,
                      Lunged at Pop's cigar—and wrecked it.
                      I viewed results with exultation:
                      Her plan had had a long **gestation**.

GIST　　　　　*main point*

Madge, Istanbul is just the place for father.
The **gist** is, there he won't be so much bother.

Caution!　　　*The **g** is soft, like **j** in **j**ig**g**le,*
*Quite different from the **g**'s in **g**i**gg**le.*

———————

GLA·cier　　*a large body of ice moving down or outward*
on land surface.

Doug, lace your snowshoes tight and start out
　　　hiking.
You'll cross the **glacier** yet—but not by
　　　biking.

Caution!　　　*Say "lace your" quickly when you speak*
*To give the **sure** sound that we seek.*

gnaw

GNAW   *to bite or chew*

      <u>Gna</u>ughty Nancy likes to be alone.
      She'll sit for hours just **gnaw**ing on a bone.

—————————

GNOME   *a subterranean dwarf of folklore*

      In <u>Nome</u>, a **gnome** awoke her with a kiss:
      An omen, so she thought, of future bliss.
      (But in truth, he meant it for her little sis.)

gratis (3)   *free of charge*

(1) GRAT·is   The <u>greatest</u> things in life are free—
There's **gratis** surf for you and me.

(2), (3) GRAT·is   Two more ways seem quite a lot,
But **grat** can rhyme with **hat** or **hot**.

————————

GRIEV·ous   *showing or causing grief*

—What **grievous** times most deeply <u>grieve
us</u>?
—It's when our last illusions leave us.

————————

Halloween (2)   *October 31, observed with tricks and
treats in the U.S.*

(1) HALL·o·**WEEN**   <u>Hal, oh! wean</u> your little girl away
From **Halloween** adventures in the hay.

(2) HALL·o·**WEEN**   <u>Holl, oh! wean</u> your little boy away
From **Halloween** adventures in the hay.

————————

HALVE   *to cut in half*

Your fiscal year can <u>have</u> a happy end:
Just **halve** the cash you'd like to spend.

Caution!   *Make the **v** sound loud and clear.
You'll impress all those who hear.*

HEI·nous   *hatefully evil*

Hey! nostalgia's really got you down,
But **heinous** crimes took place in your
hometown.

———————————

heirloom

HEIR·LOOM   *something of special value handed from one generation to another*

Visions in the air loom overhead—
The **heirloom**s I shall get when Auntie's
dead.

HE·lix   *a spiral object; a genus of snail*

See Toby—<u>he licks</u> only Daisy's hand
And her new ***Helix*** snail. He thinks they're
    grand.

––––––––––––

HELP   *to assist*

A gloom like <u>hell p</u>ervades the city!
You cannot **help?** Then give your pity.

Caution!   *Be sure you clearly sound the **l**.*
The way you do in "Ring the bell"
Or as you sigh it in "farewell."

––––––––––––

herb (2)   *a plant valued for its medicinal, savory, or*
aromatic qualities

(1) HERB   This drug will <u>curb</u> your eagerness to drink.
Oh, for an **herb** to teach you how to think.

(2) HERB   <u>Herb</u> has **herbs** to cure his every ill,
So he takes them with his every pill.

––––––––––––

HER·pes   *any of several virus diseases in which blisters*
are formed on the skin

<u>HER peas</u> truly are as sweet as wine.
Does she have **herpes**? No concern of mine!

Caution!   *Be sure to **zzzz** the **s** of peas*
*Just like the **s** of pretty pleazzzzzzzzze.*

hi·**AT**·us

a lapse in continuity

L<u>high ate us</u> in the latest game.
A sad **hiatus** in our march to fame.

---

hirsute (2)

hairy

(1) **HIR**·SUTE

Wearing <u>HER suit</u> from Macy's basement
The **hirsute** female poses in yon casement.

(2) hir·**SUTE**

If you should slip and stress just **SUTE**,
There'll be no soul to rouse dispute.

---

homage (2)

a ceremony in which a person pays deep
respect to another person

(1) **HOM**·age

<u>Ah! Midge</u> told me you were lately seen
Paying **homage** to the new May Queen.
Say what happened next—but keep it clean.

(2) **HOM**·age

To say this word just like your Ma,
Simply change the **Ah!** to **Ha!**

HOM·i·ly

a religious discourse; sermon

<u>Ha—mulling</u> over his Sunday **homily**
Our pastor found a serious anomaly.

HOS·pit·al·IZE   *to put into a hospital*

"We're glad to **hospitalize** you," said the
    nurse.
"But first the <u>hospital eyes</u> the size of your
    purse."

Caution!   *If you fail to make the zzzz of –ize,*
         *You'll have **ice** instead of **eyes**.*

HOV·er   *flutter in the air near a place*

<u>Huh! Ve</u>racity makes me grant
I **hover** over my well-heeled aunt,
Hoping she'll pay for the things I can't.

99

hubris

hubris	*assuming the power of a deity; excessive pride; arrogance toward the gods*
HU·bris	Hugh bristled, visibly angry and tense, "Me? Guilty of **hubris**, that classic offense?"

---

humane (2)	*demonstrating sympathy and pity*
(1) **hu**·**MANE**	You mayn't accept my use of "mayn't," But be **humane**, accept my "ain't."
(2) **hu**·**MANE**	Hugh may not be, right now, so much in need of money As of a female voice **humane** enough to call him "Honey."

HUN·dred   *100*

The <u>Hun, dread</u> author of a **hundred** horrid
     crimes,
May strike again if we forget his life and
     times.

Caution!   *Say all those letters, **D-R-E**,*
*And at the end slap on the **D**.*

———————

HURR·i·CANE   *a tropical cyclone*

She fashioned <u>her a cane</u> from a stout branch
After a **hurricane** destroyed her ranch
And picked a path across the avalanche.

———————

ichor (2)   *a fluid that took the place of blood in the veins*
of the Greek gods

(1) **I**·chor   When <u>I</u> corrected little Herman's spelling,
We worked on "**ichor**" 'til he started yelling.

(2) **I**·CHOR   A simple matter of either/or:
End the word with **cur** or **cor**.

IDES   *in ancient Rome, the fifteenth day of certain months, the thirteenth of others*

Woe to that man who, on the **Ides** of March,
Dec<u>ides</u> to fight beneath the Roman arch.

Caution!   *If you fail to sound the **s** as **z**,*
*You'll surely make the **d** a **t**.*

---

impasse

IM·PASSE   *an impassable road or situation*

When I saw <u>HIM pass</u>, then I knew—
In every **impasse** he'll get through.

IM·pi·ous

irreverent; lacking respect for authority

Wimpy, a scoundrel, is getting the birch
For his **impious** laughter all during church.

Caution!

This is peculiar, we have to confess,
But that first syllable gets the stress.

---

im·PUTE

to charge with, ascribe

The organ pealed. In that dim pew Tallulah's
    daughter primly sat.
Do not **impute** to God my thoughts about her
    new gosh-awful hat.

---

in·ANE

lacking significance, meaning, or point

In angels surely we arouse disdain:
We're always wicked, thoughtless, or **inane**.

---

in·CEN·di·AR·y

tending to excite or inflame

Lynn, send Dee airy messages on wings of
    dragonflies.
To crush her **incendiary** talk as a pack of lies.

Caution!

The s of lies must sound like zzzz and not like
    s in slice,
So Dee's inflaming talk won't seem a pack of
    lice.

103

in·**DICT**	*to charge with an offense*
	Sadly I watched the boss <u>indite</u> a letter: "You'll be **indict**ed if you don't do better."
Caution!	*"Indict, indite" – two words so different in their spelling and their meaning! When you have learned **indite** (to write), your pride may get to be o'erweening.*

---

in·**DITE**	*to write a formal document*
	<u>Min die t</u>o the world? I hardly think She's really ready to give up mink. I've heard, each year the girl **indite**s With care her personal Bill of Rights.
Caution!	*To remember how to spell **indite**, Just end it as its meaning—wr**ite**.*

---

inquiry (3)	*a request for information; investigation*
(1) in·**QUIR**·y	—Please <u>inquire re:</u> Ben's unanswered letter. —A regular **inquiry** would be better.
(2) **IN**·quir·y	They say that some medics <u>link worry</u> to snow. There'll be an **inquiry** to see what they know.
(3) **IN**·QUIR·y	<u>In choir, 'e</u> went from tenor to base. **Inquiry** showed it wasn't the case.

in·**SIN**·u·ATE *to introduce an idea in a subtle or indirect way*

Wallowing <u>in sin, you ate</u> forbidden fruit.
Don't you dare **insinuate** you think it's cute.

---

in·**SUR**·ance *a guarantee against loss*

I've long b<u>een sure uns</u>elfish actions
Could cut **insurance** costs to fractions.

Caution! *Ensure a future of success*
*By giving **sure** the only stress.*

---

inure (2) *to become accustomed even though painful*

(1) in·**URE** I'm <u>in YOUR</u> face; you're in MINE.
Love **inure**s—though not sublime.

(2) in·**URE** If you ever feel unsure,
You can drop the **y** of **y**our.

---

inured (2) *habituated, accustomed*

(1) in·**URED** <u>In your</u> degenerate haunt of every vice,
You've grown **inured** to license, lust, and
        lice.
And yet, you wouldn't leave at any price!

(2) in·**URED** Maybe more folks (maybe fewer)
Change <u>in your</u> into <u>in newer</u>.

I·**TAL**·ian

a native or inhabitant of Italy; a person of Italian descent

Joe h<u>it Al? Ya n</u>ever know
How far **Italian** feuds will go.

———————

i·**TAL**·ics

a typestyle with slanting characters

Did Don h<u>it Al? Ex</u>cited lookers-on
Shout in **italics**: *It began with Don!*

———————

JET·sam

cargo cast overboard to lighten the load

Our <u>jet some</u> crewmen tried to save
By throwing **jetsam** to a wave.

———————

JO·**COSE**

given to joking

<u>Joe coas</u>ted down the hill with Princess Alice.
Jocose remarks were soon to reach the palace.

———————

LAISS·ez **FAIRE**

to abstain from interference

Your mode<u>l essay fair</u>ly well explains
Our **laissez-faire**—its drawbacks and its
          gains.

Caution!

*To pronounce this word as <u>lazy fairy</u>
To the French sounds pretty scary.*

106

largesse

largesse (3)	*generous gifts*

(1) **LAR**·gesse

The <u>largest</u> return that I ever acquired
Was the **largesse** I got on the day I retired.

(2) **LAR**·gesse

When **LAR** is stressed, don't shake your fist:
Gesse can also match the sound in **gist**.

(3) lar·**GESSE**

GESSE should sound like **ZHES** or **JESS**
When syllabus two receives the stress.

LAIR   *the resting or living place of wild animals*

I found my lover in the torch's <u>glare,</u>
Hiding in a cheetah's **lair**
Combing out its matted hair.

LI·a·ble   *obligated legally or ethically*

A <u>lie a bull</u> across the pasture said
Made the liar **liable** for all the bull he spread.

---

li·**BI**·do   *psychological term for sexual drive*

Let Fathi Twa<u>lib bead O</u>phelia's hair
But stifle all **libido** of the pair.

Caution!   *As "laxative" is more polite than "purge,"*
"Libido's" more polite than "sexual urge."

LIEGE   *feudal lord*

—<u>Lee,</u> just hold your tongue and go away.
– My **liege,** my heart is sad, but I obey.

LIN·e·age   *stock, race*

<u>Lynney e</u>jected the ladies of a rather humble
    stock.
But surely, people's **lineage** is a foolish thing
    to mock.

lissome

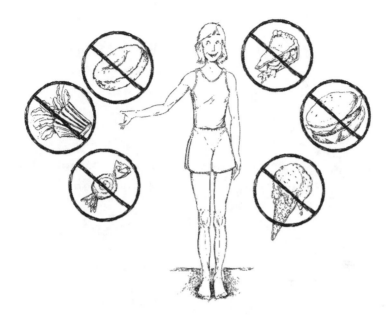

LIS·some   *lithe and limber*

B<u>liss some</u> find in smoking pot,
Some in rock and riot.
I—in my **lissome** shape—got
By sticking to my diet.

LITHE   *limber and lissome*

Here is the <u>lie the</u> speaker told:
You'll still be **lithe** when you are old.

Caution!   *So you'll never ever go astray,*
*Voice **T-H** like those in **th**em and **th**ey.*

LOLL

to recline or to move in an indolent manner

This girl's a lollapalooza, my grandpa used to say.
It means she **loll**ed about the streets in quite a tempting way.

———————

ly·CÉE

French secondary school

Lee sated his thirst o'er a year and a day
On wines he'd brought home from his Paris **lycée**.

———————

LYR·ic

music expressing personal emotion

The leer Rick bestowed on the **lyric** soprano
Prompted the tenor to smash the piano.

———————

MA·gi (2)

the traditional three wise men from the East who paid homage to the infant Jesus

(1) MA·gi

Kim, age, I feel, has touched you only lightly.
What **magi** keep you still so smart and sprightly?

(2) MA·gi

Dear Madge, I fear you've failed to see
Your crèche lacks **magi** two and three.

Caution!

*In the Midwest, number 2's preferred.
Number 1, in fact, is seldom heard!*

MAINT·en·ance   *upkeep*

> Em ain't a nun, so her **maintenance** soon
> We'll see taken up by a local tycoon.

---

malign

ma·**LIGN**   *evil in nature or effect*

> Emma lined up all infernal forces,
> Placed a curse **malign** on Papa's horses,
> So they'd fail in all their jockeyed courses.

111

mature (3) *having completed natural growth and development; grown-up*

(1) ma·**TURE** De<u>rmott, you're</u> a braggart and a bother,
And not **mature** enough to be a father.

(2) ma·**TURE** Ma<u>ma, chewer</u> of the grossest fat,
Should try to be more **mature** than that.

(3) ma·**TURE** Ma<u>ma, tour</u> the Isles without your kids,
None **mature** enough to deal with quids.

———————

MAUVE *a moderate purple, violet, or lilac color*

<u>Moe, v</u>anilla wafers, colored **mauve** and pink,
May make your kisses sweeter, but can hardly
make you think.

———————

mayoral (2) *relating to an official elected as head of a city*

(1) **MAY**·or·al <u>May Earl</u> do what has to be done
Short of his having to hire a gun.
(**Mayoral** duties are not often fun).

(2) may·**OR**·al <u>May Oral</u> do what must be done
Just short of having to hire a gun.
Most **mayoral** duties are not fun.

miasma (2)   *a heavy, noxious atmosphere*

(1) mi·**ASMA**

<u>My asthma</u> worsened when we had a romp
Within the dark **miasma** of the swamp.

(2) mi·**ASMA**

Trust <u>me, asthma</u> worsens when we romp
Within the dark **miasma** of the swamp.

———————

MIEN   *bearing, way of carrying oneself*

Bart was born on this <u>mean</u> street. His mother
    took in boarders.
Still his **mien** is that of one who daily issues
    orders.

———————

MIN·u·**ET**   *an old-fashioned slow and graceful dance*

—I fear, dear <u>Min, you et</u> the dog food by
    mistake.
—Oh, well, the dog is welcome to devour my
    ginger cake.
The creature does a **minuet** 'most every time I
    bake.

Caution!   *If you like a solid bet,*
*Always stress the final **ET**.*

minutiae (6)   *minor or minute details (plural of minutia)*

(1) mi·**NU**·ti·AE   —Your fancy woman robbed my house, you
                                           cur,
                              You ver<u>min, you! She </u>even stole my fur!
                              —Of course! I leave the **minutiae** to her!

(2, 3, 4, 5, 6)   To give you five more ways to say this word
                              Would carry "minutiae" to its most absurd.

_____

MIS·cel·**LA**·ny   *a collection of various or unrelated items*

                              <u>Miss Elainey</u> isn't really brainy.
                              She knows a lot, but it's a **miscellany**!

_____

mnemonics (2)   *a technique for aiding the memory*

(1) mne·**MON**·ics   <u>Numb, onyx</u> hunters take a break
                              To share **mnemonics** with their cakes.

(2) mne·**MON**·ics   In careful speech, most folks agree
                              The **m-n-e** should have the sound of k**nee**.

modicum

MOD·i·cum   *a small portion*

—<u>Ma, Dick come</u>s each day to act as clerk
But only does a **modicum** of work.
—Perhaps he'd make a better soda jerk.

———————

mo·**ROSE**   *sullen, gloomy*

Our Ma<u>ma roas</u>ted Uncle Kirk.
She said he's just a lazy jerk.
(He's so **morose** he cannot work.)

115

mo·TIF

a recurring theme

For you, <u>Moe, tea f</u>or two is hardly thrilling
    recreation
Since money is the main **motif** of all your
    conversation.

MOUE

a little grimace

She made a <u>mou</u>sse, and then she made a
    moue.
Her famed dessert had melted into goo.

MOUSSE

a light, spongy dessert

Just as a <u>moose</u> has never eaten **mousse,**
So, too, a goose has never had a "goose."

MYR·i·ad

having innumerable elements or aspects

The s<u>meary ad</u>hesive will ruin your clothes
And spatter **myriad** spots upon your hose.
So keep it away from your beautiful toes!

Caution!

*You must pronounce the **ad** as **ud**.*
If you don't, your name is mud.

116

NA·BOB   *a provisional governor in India; a man of great wealth and prominence*

Nay, Bob, keep your cool, nor raise your hand
Against a **nabob** from a foreign land.

———————

nacre

NA·cre   *mother-of-pearl*

An acre of **nacre** the length of the coast
Is what our economy's lacking the most.

117

naiveté (2)   *unaffected simplicity*

(1) NA·ive·**TE**   <u>Nah, Eve, ta</u>ke those rosy lips away.
To tempt me so is simply **naiveté**.

(2) na·**IVE**·TE   Switching stress to **Eve**'s okay
If you keep some on the **TE**.

NAR·ra·tor   *one who recites a story*

<u>Narrate … er</u> … sing of the deeds I have
    done,
And, **narrator**, end with the greatest—my
    son.

Caution!   *Final **o-r** has the sound of **er** not **or**,*
*With one exception: that's **mentor**.*

Caution!   *Some dictionaries give a final **or**,*
But that helps spelling—nothing more!

NÉE   *used to identify a woman by her maiden name*

Lady Vandeval, **née** Katie Smith,
Says <u>nay</u> to all requests from kin and kith.

NEM·e·sis   *anyone who seems to cause our downfall*

<u>Don, Emma, Sis</u>, and I got into politics
To wreak our vengeance on Tom Hicks,
Our **nemesis**, who gave Sis forty licks.

118

NE·o·phyte   *a novice in a convent; a beginner*

No matter what my parents did,
I always was a scrappy kid.
At Papa's k<u>nee a figh</u>t began—
A **neophyte** against a man.

Caution!   *Schwa the **o** in normal speech—*
*To **oh** the **o** will cause a breach.*

---

niche

NICHE   *a recess in a wall*

You do not quiver, even for <u>an itch</u>.
You're like an antique statue in a **niche**.

British   The British simply love their quiche
They eat it in their breakfast **niche**.

119

NI·tric   *containing nitrogen*

I don't de<u>ny tric</u>ks have been planned and
            played—
Like **nitric** acid in the lemonade.

———————

nuclear (2)   *adjective meaning "powered by nuclear
                            energy"*

(1) **NU**·cle·ar   Please <u>nuke Lee, er</u>, I mean, Bob!
                            He can't say **nuclear**. Such a slob!

(2) **NU**·cle·ar   Some say **nu** and some say **nyu**.
                            Which you say is up to you.

———————

O·**BE**·si·ty   *excessive fat*

—<u>O Bea, city</u> laws say loud and clear,
Obesity isn't permitted here.
—So no more oysters in our beer.

———————

oblique (2)   *not straightforward*

(1) o·**BLIQUE**   Tom's **oblique** remarks against Ophelia's race
                            Have stamped <u>a bleak</u> despair upon her gentle
                                        face.

(2) o·**BLIQUE**   You may like **Ike** instead of **eak**,
                            But **eak**'s the sound most people seek.

OB·lo·quy   *strongly abusive language*

Sn<u>ob, luck we</u>aves a spell around you,
So **obloquy** has never found you.

O·cher   *a yellow color named after earthy clay*

<u>O, cu</u>rmudgeon, did you never sigh and
    swoon
Half drunk with love and wine, beneath an
    ocher moon?

O·di·ous   *hateful*

J<u>odi as</u>sumes that my **odious** crimes
Do not include these ridiculous rhymes.

OFF·al   *parts of an animal that are considered inedible*

Mike's eating habits seem un<u>lawful</u>;
Most body parts he eats are **offal.**

official

of·**FI**·cial   *a person who holds an office*

The <u>fish'll</u> dangle on the fishing line
'Til some **official** says it's yours or mine.

OF·ten   *frequently; many times*

<u>Off 'n'</u> on I go to see a game,
But life is **often** boring just the same.

British   Unlike you and unlike me
Brits will often sound the **t**.

O·GIVE *in a Gothic church, a pointed arch across a vault or a diagonal rib across a window*

Oh jive on. You've left me in the lurch
To trace the **ogive**s in this Gothic church.

---

ogle (2) *to stare lasciviously*

(1) **OG**·le Your lascivious stare just boggles the mind.
You **ogle** that dummy as though you were
    blind.

(2) **O**·gle The rogue'll linger on the road to Hades:
He's sure to stop and **ogle** all the ladies.

---

ol·**FAC**·to·ry *relating to the sense of smell*

The aerosol factory belches a smoke so
    intense,
It's certain to ruin a worker's **olfactory** sense.

Caution! *We hate to give you any flack,*
*But there's no schwa 'tween **ol** and **fac**.*

123

onomatopoeia (2) *naming a thing by an imitation of the sound it is associated with*

(1) ON·o·MAT·o·**POEI**·a

On a mat, a "P" attested
This was where the Princess
    rested,
She wouldn't tell her name,
    but it could be a …
Striking case of **onomatopeia**.

(2) ON·o·MAT·o·**POEI**·a

A second way to say this word?
MOTT instead of MAT is
    heard.

O·**PAQUE** *not transparent or translucent*

Oh, pay Kirk what he says you owe.
His mind's opaque. Just let him go.

O·**PINE** *to think, have an opinion*

Oh piney woods, my friends **opine**,
Will call me back for auld lang syne.

---

ordure (2) *dung, filth*

(1) **OR**·dure

George, you're …
Ordure!

(2) **OR**·dure

Tear up your credit card. I can't afford your
Expensive clothes. To me, they're simply
    ordure.

124

OR·gy

*excessive indulgence in any activity,
especially sexual*

My boyfriend took me on a pizza **orgy**.
He ate too much. That was the end of Ge<u>orgy</u>.

---

osprey (2)

a large brown and white hawk

(1) **OS**·prey

I saw the <u>boss pre</u>tend to shoot a hawk,
So he could hear the **osprey** lovers squawk.

(2) **OS**·prey

You can say this word another way
By simply changing **pre** to **pray**.

OSS·i·fy

*to change into bone; to become callous or
rigid*

B<u>oss, if I</u> can trust my practiced eye,
Your brain cells have begun to **ossify**.

Caution!

*Pronounce the **Boss** like folks back East
And praise their help at last at least.*

---

otitis (2)

inflammation of the ear

(1) o·**TI**·tis

<u>O Titus</u>, won't you let me bite your ear?
You will not get **otitis**—never fear.

(2) o·**TI**·tis

In careful speech, as said by Sis,
The **is** is like the **iss** in k**iss**.

125

PAE·an   *a hymn of praise, triumph, or thanksgiving*

I sought a curious <u>pea, un</u>known to modern
    botany,
And wrote a **paean** to it, although I never
    got 'ny.

---

paisley

PAIS·ley   *woven or printed with colorful abstract figures*

He <u>pays</u> Leona richly every Christmas season
In **paisley** pants that, like this verse, have
    neither rhyme nor reason.

126

PA·pal   *of the pope*

We <u>pay poli</u>cemen well, with great vacations.
Why should they ask for **papal** dispensations?

———————

pa·**REN**·tal   *pertaining to a parent*

<u>Papa, rental</u> fees for cars are high,
Your **parental** duty is to buy.

———————

pa·**RI**·ah   *outcast*

<u>Papa, rio</u>t if you think you must—
Driven almost mad by loot and lust,
Like all **pariah**s, you will bite the dust.

———————

PAS·tor·al   *relating to the pastor of a church or to rustic settings in literature*

Our <u>pastor al</u>lots to the usual **pastoral** chores
What time he can spare from the study of
        baseball scores.

Caution!   *Stress falls on syllable the first.*
                        On the second would be the worst!

———————

per·**FORCE**   *by force of necessity*

Your p<u>aper force</u>s me to say,
"You cannot write. So, come what may,
Perforce I must deny the A."

127

pi·**AN**·o

a stringed percussion instrument with a keyboard

Pap<u>py, Ann or</u>iginated
Where **piano** music's hated.
Happily she emigrated
And with a pianist was mated.

Caution!

Do the very best you can.
*Put the stress upon the **Ann**.*

—————

picayune (2)

small-minded, petty, trivial

(1) **PIC**·a·YUNE

—Help Jeff <u>pick a un</u>icorn to keep!
—I would, but he's so **picayune**
Helping him just makes me weep.
(Besides, they're only in his sleep.)

 (2) PIC·a·**YUNE**

Perhaps we're being **picayune**,
But stress can switch from **PIC** to **YUNE**.

—————

piquant (2)

agreeably stimulating to the palate

(1) **PI**·quant

My A & <u>P cont</u>inually tells me
How pure and **piquant** are the foods it sells
     me.

(2) pi·**QUANT**

Stress the **CONT** or stress the **P**,
Either way—we all agree.

128

porcupine

PORC·u·pine   *a rodent with sharp bristles in its hair*

Old Tray, the <u>pork ya pine</u> for makes you
   sick,
So here's a roasted **porcupine** to lick!

---

prelude (3)   *introductory performance, action, or event*

(1) **PREL**·UDE   Use Suave or <u>Prell: You'd</u> look a whole lot
   better.
Right now, you look like Mama's English
   setter—
No **prelude** to a life as ace go-getter.

(2) **PRE**·lude   <u>Pray lewd</u> movies never reach our screen—
They're **prelude** to a life of acts unclean.

(3) **PRE**·lude   If you substitute the sound of **pre** for **pray**,
You'll say this word another way.

129

PROB·lem   *a source of perplexity or dilemma*

      —Can you hel<u>p Rob? Lum</u>bago's made him
            lame.
      —No **problem**. Send him back to whence he
            came.

PSALM   *a sacred song or poem*

      The <u>somb</u>er shadows of the stately palms
      Enfolded us as we intoned the **psalm**s.
      (So moved my father was, he passed out
            alms.)

Caution!   *Psalm and palm and alm*
      *All delete the **l** like calm.*

PU·ber·ty   *the period of first becoming capable of*
      reproducing sexually

      "<u>Pugh</u>!" <u>Berty</u> murmured, then started to roar,
      "Going through **puberty**'s really a chore."

puerile (4)   *childish*

(1) **PUER**·ile

I joined a <u>pure re</u>ligious sect
That never cursed, or drank, or necked.
Our **puerile** effort lived through two
        Decembers,
By which time we had lost all seven members.

(2, 3, 4)

Three more ways to say this word
Seem to us a bit absurd!
But if you want to fill your cup,
Take the time to look them up.

———————

quaff (2)   *to drink*

(1) **QUAFF**

Dun<u>k waff</u>les in tomato paste;
Then **quaff** hot tea to kill the taste.

(2) **QUAFF**

It's really only half and half,
Since **quaff** can also rhyme with **laugh**.

———————

quay (3)   *an artificial landing place beside navigable water*

(1) **QUAY**

She —the <u>key</u> to all of life for me —
Left me standing lonely on the **quay**.

(2, 3) **QUAY**

Dictionaries say (and so we must obey)
Quay can also sound like <u>quail</u> or <u>kay</u>.

131

QUICHE *a French egg dish*

The <u>key sh</u>e gave me opens her back door,
And oh! The **quiche** she makes calls out for
more!

———————

RAFF·i·a *a fiber used for making baskets and mats*

This <u>graph Ia</u>n made for the **raffia** mart
Proves that the business is falling apart.

———————

rapport (2) *a sympathetic relationship*

(1) ra·**PPORT** —I can't w<u>rap or</u>ders all day long,
Say "yes," although the boss is wrong,
And then come home and sing your song.
—Maintain **rapport** and tag along.

(2) ra·**PPORT** Since the unstressed syllable is **ra**,
No surprise, then, **a** can go to schwa.

———————

real estate (2) *land, including buildings thereon*

(1) **RE**·al e·**STATE** The farmer, so the town affirms,
Planted his fields in fishing worms.
But when hard times arrived, the <u>realist ate</u>
The lively produce of his **real estate**.

(2) **RE**·al e·**STATE** The **e** of estate a schwa can be,
Or stay as **ist** as you can see.

realtor

REAL·tor

an accredited real-estate agent

If there's a <u>real tur</u>key for Thanksgiving,
My friend, the **Realtor**, finds life worth
     living.

———————

RE·cess

a suspension of business or classes at school

My boy came home from school and said
          <u>three ses-</u>
quipedalian worms had grabbed him at **recess**.

Caution!

*Of course the child had really heard
Someone say "sesquipedalian word"
(One that's hollow, long, or just absurd.)*

133

regalia (2)   *emblems or insignia of rank, office, or membership*

(1) re·**GAL**·i·a   You may <u>rig alien</u> armies for the battle,
                         And add **regalia** 'til their medals rattle.
                         I still prefer my trusty atl-atl.

(2) re·**GAL**·ia   Syllables can go from four to three?
                         If you do, it's quite okay with me.

───────

REG·i·men   *a systematic course of therapy, such as a diet*

                         <u>Redge, a mon</u>key fills its guts
                         On a **regimen** of nuts.
                         Staying fit (no "ands" or "buts").

───────

REG·u·lar   *ordered according to some established principle*

                         <u>Greg, ya lur</u>k in all my dreams.
                         You're a **regular** feature of all my schemes.
                         But why do ya use those smelly creams?

───────

rendezvous (3)   *a meeting*

(1) **REN**·dez·vous   <u>Ron, Dave oo</u>zes blood from ears and nose:
                         He kept a **rendezvous** with his sister's foes.

(2, 3, 4)   Pay attention to the **d** plus **e**.
                         They can also rhyme with **duh**, **dĭ**, **dee**.

134

RES·pite   *a reprieve or brief repose*

In your lecture, Dr. Sands,
Stress pituitary glands.
But grant a **respite** when you're through,
Read us a line of verse or two.

_____

reverend (2)   *a member of the clergy*

(1) **REV·**e·rend   Trevor unduly has started again on his
                                scoffing.
                            Reverend only imbibes so to stifle his
                                coughing.

(2) **REV·**e·rend   In three syllable words with the stress on the
                                first,
                            The second turns schwa—or deletes at the
                                worst.

_____

ris·**QUÉ**   *verging on impropriety or indecency*

Why does your spouse risk aging
                                prematurely?
His **risqué** jokes will doom him fast and
                                surely.

RI·tu·al   *a ceremonial action*

After I kicked your ill-disciplined kitten,
My **ritual** "sorry!" was hastily written.
You sent a reply so loaded with gall,
I'm sorry I w<u>rit you a </u>letter at all.

Caution!   *Note when **t** is followed by **you***
                    Suddenly both are easy to chew.

---

robot

robot (2)   *a humanlike mechanical being*

(1) **RO**·BOT   —I'll <u>row, but</u> we are endless miles from
                              shore.
                          —I never thought a **robot**'s arm got sore.

(2) **RO**·BOT   "G<u>row bott</u>le gourds," my **robot** pleads,
                          "I really like to eat the seeds!"

136

row

ROW *brawl, noisy disturbance*

I gather from your furrowed b<u>row</u>
We'll soon be whipping up our daily **row**.

----

saboteur (2) *a person who intentionally creates chaos*

(1) SA·bo·**TEUR** That jumping jacka<u>ss, Abba, tur</u>ned a nasty
trick:
He called me **saboteur**—and I'm afraid he
made it stick.

(2) SA·bo·**TEUR** A second way (of which we're sure),
You simply change the **tur** to **tour**.

sadist (2)   *someone who gets pleasure out of hurting*
                                  others

(1) **SA**·dist   They <u>say dist</u>orted images are rife
                                  In minds of **sadist**s as they wield the knife.

(2) **SAD**·ist   To voice this word a second way,
                                  You simply put in **sad** for **say**.

                                  _____

SAN·guine   *cheerful, confident*

                                  Tonight she <u>sang, Gwynne</u> thought, a little
                                                  better.
                                  Some **sanguine** fans reached out to pet 'er.

                                  _____

SATE   *to satisfy, satiate*

                                  <u>Sat</u>an himself couldn't hope to **sate**
                                  Mary's desire to have a blind date.
                                  Regrettably, though, she's having to wait.
                                  The poor little thing's not even seen eight.

                                  _____

SA·ti·**ATE**   *to satisfy to the fullest*

                                  You <u>say she ate</u> from dusk 'til dawn
                                  (And didn't even stop to yawn)
                                  To **satiate** her yen for prawn!

satyr (2)   *a goatlike deity of ancient Greece, given to revelry*

(1) **SA**·tyr   I could not <u>sate 'er</u> boundless appetite
Were I a **satyr** roving through the night.

(2) **SAT**·yr   A second way, there's no debate,
Is simply put in **sat** for **sate**.

Caution!   *Because it's Greek (you'll doubtless learn that later),*
*The sound of **y** is like the **e** in wait**er**.*

———————

sauterne (2)   *a sweet white table wine*

(1) sau·**TERNE**   The first time I <u>saw tern</u>s in flight,
I was so captured by delight
I sipped **sauterne** all through the night.

(2) sau·**TERNE**   This word is French, so you should know
They prefer we change the **saw** to **so**.

schedule

SCHED·ule   *a timetable or program*

If you a<u>sk Ed, you'll</u> get no satisfaction.
His **schedule** leaves no time for interaction.

––––––––––

schism (2)   *a split or division*

(1) **SCHIS**·əm   Thoma<u>s is a m</u>an who shocked the nation.
He caused a **schism** in his congregation
By banning every form of conjugation.
Only those who didn't know the word
Didn't find the ban downright absurd.

(2) **SCHIS**·əm   To say this word a second way,
You have to sound **C-H** as **K**
And let the schwa just fade away.

sci·**AT**·i·ca   *a pain in the lower back and adjacent parts*

Cy, Attica can best be seen on tours.
Take in the sights from towers down to
      sewers,
To lose that old **sciatica** of yours.

SCI·on   *a descendent, child*

Scions of a noble house complain,
"A sigh unheard can linger in the brain."

SCOURGE   a *cause of wide or great affliction*

It's all I ask: Urge Bill to stop and think
Before he bows beneath the **scourge** of drink.

second

SEC·ond   *a moment, instant*

The senior made a <u>second</u>ary argument for
    kissing.
It tells you in a **second** whether any teeth are
    missing.

Caution!   *What's the letter that ends this word?*
    *—It's **d**, not **t**. Be sure it's heard!*

SE·NILE   *characteristic of old age*

The sickest <u>scene I'll</u> ever see
Is **senile** you embracing teenage me.

142

SHORT-LIVED (2)   *not living or lasting long*

(1) short-LIVED   We, in <u>short, lived</u> dancing in the
                          fire—
                      Symbol of our hot **short-lived** desire.

(2) short-LIVED   As sure as **dove's** the same as **dived**,
                      Short-**lived** may also rhyme with
                          jived.

_____

SIEGE   *a military blockade of a fortified place*

                      My aged eyes <u>see</u> just enough, my liege,
                      To string my trusty bow and join the **siege**.

_____

SKEIN   *a quantity of thread or yarn wrapped in a coil*

                      Kandiss <u>Kane</u>field doesn't give a darn
                      When her kitty swipes a **skein** of yarn.

_____

SLOV·en·ly   *untidy, especially of one's dress or person*

                      Tess <u>lovin'ly</u> said, as she patted my shoulder,
                      "You'll not be so **slovenly**, dear, when you're
                          older."

143

SOLD·er   *to unite surfaces by applying a metal alloy*

It's odd Erline today signed up to learn to
solder.
Next week, no doubt, she'll quit the class for
something even odder.

Caution!   *For reasons that are hard to tell*
                              We quietly forget the l.

———————

SPEC·ter   *ghost*

The folks suspect 'er of a secret crime.
She wanders like a **specter** all the time.

———————

STA·sis   *stable state*

Stay, Sis, don't dismiss your reeling date
'Til he's in **stasis,** or a stable state.

———————

STE·la   *an upright stone slab or pillar engraved with*
                              an inscription and used as a monument

I know you'd steal a dime to earn yourself a
nickel.
But if you try to steal this **stela**—then you're
in a pickle.

144

STE·lae   *plural of stela*

Will glass and <u>steel e</u>liminate at last this
       ancient tribe,
Who on their **stelae**, myths they did inscribe?

---

surprise (2)   *(n.) taking unawares*

(1) sur·**PRISE**   <u>Sir, prize</u>d are beds that let you sleep.
       It's no **surprise** they don't come cheap.

(2) sur·**PRISE**   You'll note two **r**'s adorn this word.
       Make sure at least the second's heard.

---

surprise (2)   *(v.) to strike with wonder or amazement*

(1) sur·**PRISE**   Yes, <u>sir, prize</u>s soon will be awarded.
       Some may **surprise** you, sir. Our taste is
       sordid.

(2) sur·**PRISE**   In **surprise**, the **r**'s are two.
       Omit the first? It's up to you.

---

surrogate (2)   *substitute*

(1) **SURR·**o·GATE   —<u>Sir, Rug Eight</u>-Oh-Eight I cannot sell
       you.
       —You go to hell! No **surrogate** will do.

(2) **SURR·**o·gate   If you substitute a **get** for **gate**.
       You'll still impress your date or mate.

SYC·o·phan·cy   *fawning (obsequious) flattery*

If overdone and <u>sick o' fun, see</u> Moriarty.
He'll hold a spelling bee or quilting party.
No **sycophancy** there.
No need to comb your hair.

———————

tacit (2)   *unspoken but approving*

(1) **TAC**·it   <u>TASS</u> attests to supporting our plan
By its **tacit** approval of aid to Iran.

Caution!   *In normal speech (no "and" or "but"),*
*The **it** of "tac**it**" sounds like **ut**.*

(2) **TAC**·it   If you rhyme the **it** with sp**it**,
In careful speech, you'll be a hit.

———————

TAC·i·turn   *temperamentally disinclined to talk*

His affection is <u>tacit. Earn</u> money he can.
But why did she wed such a **taciturn** man?

———————

THE·a·ter   *a place where plays or movies are presented*

Miss <u>Thea tur</u>ned a brilliant pink
When asked what **theater**goers think.
She answered with a hint of gall,
"What makes you think they think at all?"

titular (2)   *having the title without the functions of an office*

(1) **TIT**·u·lar   A <u>stitch'll ar</u>rest that run in your stocking
                             Our **titular** bishop considers so shocking.

(2) **TIT**·u·lar   There is another way to say this word;
                             However, it is very seldom heard.

---

topographic (2)   *portraying the configuration of an area, showing the position of roads, waterways, cities, etc.*

(1) TOP·o·**GRAPH**·ic   Let's <u>stop a graphic</u> nude display
                             By throwing our TVs away.
                             We'll build a **topographic** map with
                                 clay.

Caution!   *Begin this word by thinking of a **top**. Then **topographic** comes before you stop.*

(2) TO·po·**GRAPH**·ic   If you say **t-o** as **toe**,
                             All will think you're in the know!

---

tou·**CHÉ**   *used to acknowledge a hit in fencing or the success of an argument*

                             —This spot's <u>too sha</u>dy for a bed of roses.
                             —And so are you, the government discloses.
                             —**Touché**. You're smarter than the world
                                 supposes.

147

TUSK   *a long protruding tooth*

—This wall <u>Tusc</u>an art adorns.
That wall holds our **tusk**s and horns.
Another, shapes of gnomes and Norns.
—Let's stop! I've got to rest my corns.

––––––––––

VA·grant   *wandering about*

"To Bill please con<u>vey</u>," <u>grunt</u>s **vagrant**
       Alice,
"My best regards—with one large dash of
       malice."

––––––––––

valet (2)   *a man's male servant who performs personal*
services

(1) **VAL·**et   <u>Val, lay</u> out your husband's clothes.
Valet wives get no repose.

(2) va·**LET**   Stress the **Val** or stress the **lay**—
Folks accept it either way.

––––––––––

VER·te·bra   *any of a number of bones composing the*
spinal column

A<u>vert a bru</u>sh with yonder cop
And bury this **vertebra** found by pop.

148

vertebrae (2)   *the bony segments composing the spinal*
                      column; plural of vertebra

(1) **VER**·te·BRAE   You must a<u>vert a brea</u>ch of promise claim.
                      Stiffen your **vertebrae**, reject the blame.

(2) **VER**·te·BRAE   To say this word a second way,
                      You simply rhyme the **brae** with **bray**.

---

via

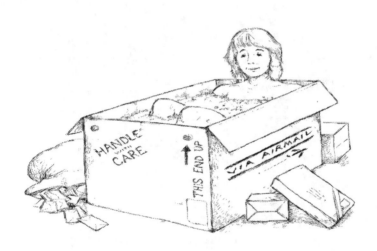

via (2)   *by way of*

(1) **VI**·a   Even not having a dress,
                      Li<u>vy a</u>rrived **via** Postal Express.

(2) **VI**·a   The woman bought a <u>vial</u> of a dark and
                          nameless lotion.
                      That night she made her exit **via** this noxious
                          potion.

vicarious

vicarious (2)	*experienced or suffered by one person as a substitute for another*
(1) VI·**CAR**·i·ous	<u>Vy, Cary</u> asserts that when somebody's injured or ill, You can sit by their bedside and catch a **vicarious** chill.
(2) vi·**CAR**·i·ous	A second way is often heard: The **vic** of **vic**tory starts the word.

vice versa (2)   *with the order changed*

(1) **VI**·ce **VER**·sa   The <u>vice a versa</u>tile modern statesman
                    needs
            Is skill to win a vote with words, not
                    deeds,
            Or **vice versa** if it fits his needs.

(2) **VI**·ce **VER**·sa   Unwritten **a** you can with friends
                    delete—
            But not when talking to the world's elite.

WAN·der   *to move about without a fixed course or aim*

Wave your <u>wand, Er</u>line, for over yonder
I see the evil spirits wail and **wander**.
Who can tell the sordid things they ponder.

WITH   *alongside*

You say we'll <u>with</u>er in these desert sands
With or without the help of native bands.

Caution!   ***T-H** is voiced, so let me hear it!*
Louder still! Now that's the spirit.

151

wither

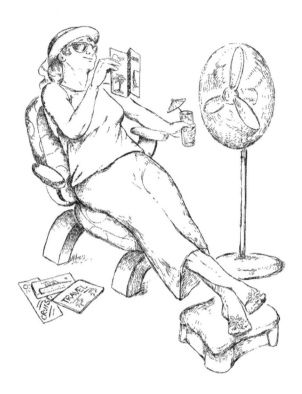

WITH·er   *to become dry and sapless; to lose vitality, force, or freshness*

I'd wander <u>with Earl</u>'s sis to foreign lands,
But she would **wither** in those desert sands.

———

WIZ·ened   *dried up, shriveled*

This final <u>quiz und</u>oubtedly will show
What all you weary, **wizened** seniors know.
In heaven, are we obliged to shovel snow?

WON·der　　　　　*to feel surprise, curiosity, or doubt*

You <u>won dire</u>ct applause from foreign
　　　nations?
I **wonder** if you offered reparations!

Caution!　　　　　*An issue that we dare not skirt:*
　　　　　　　　　　*The sound of **dir** is that of **dir**t.*

———————

WOR·ship　　　　*to honor as a divine being*

There <u>were ship</u>s there. If we catch up with
　　　them,
Tonight we'll **worship** in Jerusalem.

———————

WOULD·n't　　　*negative of the auxiliary expressing wish or*
　　　　　　　　　　intent

The natives placed upon a <u>wooden t</u>restle
The heads of all the men who **wouldn't**
　　　wrestle.

———————

WRES·tle　　　　*to take part in a violent struggle*

That simple <u>dress'll</u> do for every day,
Unless your boyfriend **wrestles** it away.

Xan·**THIPP**·e   *the wife of Socrates*

Ta<u>rzan, Tippy</u> bright and bold,
Identified **Xantippe** as a scold.

YOLK   *the yellow of an egg*

These gourmet eggs will keep the <u>yoke</u>ls up
    all night,
Whether our rustic guests prefer the **yolk** or
    white.